A TIME OF
MADNESS

A TIME OF
MADNESS

A Memoir of Partition

SALMAN RASHID

ALEPH

ALEPH

ALEPH BOOK COMPANY
An independent publishing firm
promoted by *Rupa Publications India*

First published in India in 2017
by Aleph Book Company
7/16 Ansari Road, Daryaganj
New Delhi 110 002

ISBN: 978-93-84067-36-6

1 3 5 7 9 10 8 6 4 2

Printed and bound in India by Replika Press Pvt. Ltd.

Dedicated to all those Hindus, Sikhs and Muslims
who lost their worldly possessions
and sometimes their lives
for the creation of Pakistan

ONE

On the twentieth day of March 2008, I headed home for the first time in my life. I was fifty-six years and a month old. Walking east across the border gates at Wagah, I was on my way to the fulfilment of a family pietas of very long standing. I was going to a home I had never known; a home in a foreign land, a land that state propaganda wanted me to believe was enemy territory. But I knew it as a country where my ancestors had lived and died over countless generations. That was the home where the hearth kept the warmth of a fire first kindled by a matriarch many hundred years, nay, a few thousand years, ago and which all of a sudden had been extinguished in a cataclysm in 1947.

In that great upheaval, in a singular moment in time, that home ceased to be home. One part of the family made it across the border to become a tiny part of a huge data: they were among the nearly two million people uprooted from their homes. Another part of the family also became a statistic—a grim and ghastly one: they were part of the more than one million unfortunate souls who paid with their blood for the division of India and foundation of the new country of Pakistan for Muslims. They who died were not just Muslims who lived east of the new line drawn by Cyril Radcliffe. They were Sikhs, Hindus and even Jains who had homes thousands of years old, west of this line in the land that became Pakistan.

Born four years and six months after the dreadful event, I had grown up in a home where we only knew in an amorphous, indirect sort of way that the family had suffered terribly in what the elders referred to as Partition. Even though the lost ones were referred to from time to time, no one ever spoke explicitly of the loss and how it may have occurred. The inhumanity of man against fellow man, of neighbours slaughtering those with whom they shared a common wall, was never spoken of. Never was it mentioned that some may have survived and, forced to convert to another faith, may still be living in India. This last thought was simply too much to take for these damaged but proud Muslim minds.

I did not know it as a child, but I now understand that they simply did not wish to recall the loss of parents, sisters, a grandparent and a home. I wonder if it was because my father, his brother and the one surviving sister were afraid that talking of that time would shatter their apparently unbreakable veneer of stoic self-control. Were they afraid the mention of the loss of Partition would bring tears?

I remember being told by my mother that my father was known to have never wept. Not even as a child. But one wintry day in late 1960 he asked for boiled potatoes before lunch. I remember him peeling the potatoes and sprinkling them with salt and black pepper and biting into them, still piping hot. As he was eating the potatoes, he casually mentioned how his own father had loved them like this. Later my mother said she had seen his eyes mist.

That was the only indication of grief associated with the memory of Partition, the home in Jalandhar and all those who had once lived there and had failed to make it across Radcliffe's line. Before that and long afterwards it was as if my father, the eldest, and his siblings had sworn upon themselves an omertà of sorts regarding the years before August 1947. In our home in Lahore, we only had a handful of sepia images taken by my father, no mean photographer himself, of the family, both on the maternal and paternal sides. We had no images of Railway Road in Jalandhar where the home stood. Of the interior of the house, we have one of my grandfather, relaxing in a chair in the courtyard with potted plants and creepers in the background, and one of my father in tweed jacket and tie, hands in his pockets, striking a Shyam Saigal pose on the stairs. Nor were there images of the ancestral home in Ughi, the village where the extended family congregated from time to time.

In all the years of television shows in which so-called heroes of the independence movement would hog the screen and scream themselves hoarse regaling the audience with details of the great services they and their families had rendered for the homeland, there was never a word from either my father or uncle, Habib ur Rehman (whom we affectionately called 'Chan'—an abbreviation of the traditional form of address, Chacha Jan), about anything they had done for the country. With everyone else falling over themselves citing the sacrifices they had made in terms of the vast properties (they were always vast!) lost on the other side of the border, my family remained steadfastly silent. They never evoked the tragedy that had befallen them in Jalandhar and never referred to the loss of whatever was once theirs as sacrifice.

As a child in the Lahore of early 1960s, I often heard friends talking of the lands and havelis their families had to abandon in India. In order not to be left wanting in this exchange, I once asked my father what sort of haveli our grandfather owned.

'Your grandfather owned no haveli. He had a modest house measuring seventeen marlas.' (The marla, a Punjabi measure of land area, equals roughly 19 square metres.)

I do not remember if I was disappointed, but I do know I told my friends we did not own havelis in Jalandhar. Though some might have pitied me, I do not recall if I was made fun of. Among the children of all those wealthy immigrants from Jalandhar, I was the only one whose family was seemingly badly off in the old country.

The family may have had reason for holding their silence. Those who perished in the home in Railway Road died alone. No word was ever heard of what exactly had transpired. I am certain that my father and his siblings would have hoped against hope for some months after August 1947 to hear that the rest of the family was alive and well in a refugee camp somewhere and that that they would soon be on their way to a reunion with everyone else. But hope is not eternal. Certainly not in cases like that of the Partition of India.

In November 1996, Chan gave voice for the first and only time to the grief he held within his soul. One morning we received word by telephone from Rawalpindi that Zubeda phuphi, my paternal aunt, had been murdered in her home. The family had only shortly before hired a Kashmiri man to help around in the house. That morning my phupha (uncle) and my cousin had gone out for a while. On returning, as they drove up the driveway, they saw the servant leaving the house.

Nothing seemed untoward and my uncle assumed he had been sent out on an errand. The first chilling sign of the horror that had taken place in their absence were the footsteps stained in blood, leading out of my uncle and aunt's bedroom. There on the floor in a pool of fresh blood my aunt lay dead, her throat slit. Nearby lay the kitchen knife. The cupboard was open and had been rifled through. Later my uncle found that all the man could think of stealing was the packet containing the ownership documents of the house. Little did he know that the papers were of no use to him. In the servant's room the man had calmly changed from his blood-stained clothes, still hanging on a peg, into the shalwar suit he was seen in as he left the house.

The picture that emerged was that my aunt, then seventy-three and rather frail, had been working in the kitchen, while the servant was dusting the rooms. At some point she must have heard some suspicious noise from her bedroom and with the knife she was using still in her hands, she went out to investigate. The man would then have been looking in the cupboard and upon being surprised, snatched the knife out of my aunt's hand and slit her throat. She did not stand a chance.

That afternoon, us men having returned from the graveyard after the burial, were sitting around, still numbed by the tragedy. No one was talking when Chan said, 'We lost two sisters in Jalandhar during the Partition riots, and she who made it through virtually from under the swords of rioters got to Pakistan only to be murdered in her own home by her servant.'

Chan's voice did not waver. I did not spot the sheen of a tear in his eyes. Though the vow of silence was broken, that to never shed a tear was kept. As I blinked away the tears by staring at the darkness outside the window, I realized why Partition was never mentioned in our family. Neither my father nor Chan, nor indeed during her lifetime, had Zubeda phuphi ever talked of that time because the memory was simply too horrific. Silence was their way of keeping the enormous grief at bay; that was their way of struggling to forget an abiding memory that refused to be forgotten. Now with this tragedy fresh upon us, Chan gave voice to his distress.

Later, as our car was reversing out of my aunt's home, I watched her husband and Chan, childhood friends, standing together looking evenly at the car carrying the rest of us away to Lahore. That was when I broke down. I fought hard to control myself, but my face contorted in a grimace before the flood came. Holding my head very still and stifling the sob that tried to break through, I wept very quietly because I did not want my father in the back to know.

That Chan had mentioned Partition was for me the first indication that he had suffered deeply and still suffered. To this day I have not been able to figure if my tears were from the grief of the horrible murder that November day or from Chan's reference to the terrible loss of Partition.

Back in the 1950s my maternal aunt would sometimes tell us children stories of life in Jalandhar, but I was too young at the time to fully comprehend or even recollect them. The one thing we were told repeatedly was that our grandfather, Dr Badaruddin, a doctor, was utterly free of prejudice towards followers of other faiths. That he treated all his patients with the same affection and attention. Rauha, my elder sister, remembered other things too and from her, years later, I learned some remarkable facts.

In 1985, when I lived in Karachi, Abdul Haq, a cousin of

my mother's, who had been brought up in my grandfather's home in Jalandhar, returned to that town for the first time since Partition. He came back with a 35-mm colour print showing a part of Railway Road bordered by houses. The image he gave my parents had a house in the middle with a penned arrow pointing to it. That was my first impression of the home my grandfather had named Habib Manzil after Chan. Upon seeing the picture, the first thought that occurred to me and to which I gave no voice was: if only history had taken another turn, we would still have been living in this house!

Back in the early 1960s, we had a visitor from Jalandhar, my maternal uncle Abdussalam's childhood friend Ramesh. He stayed with us for a few days and he was mamu to us, the same as our own uncle. He called my mother Apa and my father Bhaijan, just as my uncle did. Then my uncle, visiting from Lyallpur where he taught in a college, and Ramesh mamu were driven to my aunt's home in Lahore cantonment. The visit of an Indian Hindu to the cantonment of what was even then a security state was kept a closely guarded secret, with us children instructed to only call him mamu. Never were we to utter his name lest it be heard by some military type and the family be arrested for harbouring an enemy spy. This may have just been misplaced fear, but that was clearly how citizens in a state growing increasingly paranoid behaved.

It was perhaps because of this episode that despite my seven years in the army during the 1970s and despite state propaganda convincing us of India being the enemy, I was surprisingly free of any prejudice for those across the border. In fact, if there was a country I wanted to visit, it was India. In the 1980s, less than a decade out of the army, I was told there was no way I could travel east of the border because of my military past. Then in 1997, on the fiftieth anniversary of Partition, Beena Sarwar, my friend and editor at the *News on Sunday*, told me to apply for a visa since everyone on either side with any connection to the other was going across to write Partition stories.

Beena spoke with someone at the Indian High Commission in Islamabad and instructed me to see this person with my passport and filled in forms. Filling those horrendous five-page forms asking for tedious details was soul-destroying business— and in quintuplicate (no carbon paper, please)—yet the lure of India made me do it. I got into the waiting hall inside the High Commission all right, but never got to see the gentleman Beena had spoken with.

In the waiting hall, stuffy in the August heat with a few dozen expectant applicants, there were two uniformed men, probably peons—one a mousy type, the other a big-boned muscular bouncer type with a vermilion tilak on his forehead. From time to time, the big man barked rather rudely at people to keep to their seats. Since all seats were taken, I was standing to one side when he completely surprised me. He asked a younger man to vacate his chair and, coming up to me, very civilly addressing me as 'sahib', asked me to take it. When everyone else's papers were collected, but mine surprisingly were not, the Bouncer came to me and said, 'Sahib, I suggest you leave, you are not getting a bija.'

I asked to see the gentleman I was supposed to meet and the man said it was he who had instructed him to tell me to make myself scarce. I protested about my papers not even being looked at and the man hinted that was for the better. I refused to leave. A little while later the man very firmly told me I was wasting my time. It was beyond comprehension why I should be singled out like this and it took eleven years for me to understand how I had been favoured. In 2008, applying again, I realized that by not entertaining my papers, the High Commission had not put me on record as having been refused, a major hindrance in subsequent attempts for a visa. By official record, I had never applied.

In late February 2008, my wife Shabnam and I were invited to dinner at the home of the Indian High Commissioner. We walked into the living room and as Satyabrata Pal and his wife came forward to greet us, I spoke even before either could utter a word of welcome. I said, 'Do you know yours is the only country to ever deny me a visa?'

It turned out that the High Commissioner was a regular reader of my weekly history column which appeared, at the time, in the widely-read English daily *Daily Times*, as well as of my work as a travel writer. Pal did not know of my connection with Jalandhar and very briefly I told him all I knew of the events of August 1947 and my desire to pick up whatever was left of the fast-disappearing spoor of that long ago upheaval. The good man instructed me to send him my papers as soon as I got back to Lahore.

And so, in March that year, sixty-one years after Partition, I got my first ever Indian visa. For readers in any country other than our two neighbouring states it would sound strange, but Pakistanis and Indians only get city-specific visas and are not permitted free run on the other side of the common border. Both countries hamper visitors with requirements of reporting to the police when entering or leaving a city and travellers are known to be hassled or even arrested if found in a city not specified on the visa. Even the choice of port of entry and exit is restricted: one must enter and leave by the same port and the same mode of transport. However, my passport was stamped to enable me to visit Amritsar, Jalandhar, the ancestral village of Ughi, Delhi and Solan without police reporting. The special treat was that I could cross the border between Wagah on our side and Attari on the Indian by foot. I was not required to take either the tediously slow train to Attari or the long needless bus journey from Lahore to Delhi in which I would not be permitted to disembark anywhere en route.

On the morning of 20 March 2008, an elderly Indian gentleman and I were the only ones crossing the border and we sailed through the formalities on our side. On the Indian side, the official with a Rohtak accent was a very chatty type who asked me what I did for a living and said he was delighted to meet a Pakistani writer. Upon learning this was my first visit he congratulated me and asked for mithai. In Pakistan that was the traditional way of demanding a bribe and I was rather taken aback as this was the first time in all my border crossings I had faced such a situation and had no idea how to react. Handing back my passport, he looked at me expectantly. I had either Pakistani money or Indian rupees in five hundreds, so I offered him two hundred Pakistani. He said he would not know what to do with that.

In full view of his colleagues, I handed him five hundred Indian rupees and said out loud, 'Don't take it home with you. Share it with the rest of your associates.' The man whose name was either Shahbaz or Shahzad—Persian names both, meaning he was a Muslim—pocketed the money with a wide grin on his face.

Salman Rashid

'Promise me you won't write about this in your book,' said the man.

'I promise no soul other than you and I will ever hear of this,' I lied brazen-facedly. The dour expressions of his colleagues showed we were not the only ones in on this little secret.

My friend in Lahore, Mohammad Tahseen, had made arrangements for me to be picked up by a Ranjiv Sharma (Raja to his friends). But he was late to arrive and I sat at the tea stall just outside the gate on the Indian side. The serving boys came around to hound me with CDs of Indian film stars and of the rather pointless flag-lowering ceremony that takes place every evening at the border. Other than the spectacle of ridiculous goose-stepping, it is remarkable only for being animated with barefaced rancour on both sides and I confess I have never ever been in the stands crammed with spectators witnessing the silliness. But then, perhaps, I am not truly—and fashionably—nationalistic. I said no to whatever was on offer.

'Have some beer then,' said the boy.

'Beer? At ten in the morning?' I asked.

It turned out that Pakistanis hit the sauce as soon as they stepped across the border—damn the hour of the day. This was exactly what they did when they travelled to Xinjiang over the Khunjerab Pass in vast multitudes back when China first opened that border in the mid 1980s. At Pir Ali, the border post just across the pass in China, local entrepreneurs had set up stalls selling alcohol and they made a pretty penny because of thirsty Pakistani 'tourists' steeped in the hypocrisy spawned by the cock-eyed policies of that accursed duplicitous general who then ruled our sorry land.

The drunken antics of the self-proclaimed pious and terribly self-righteous Pakistanis in Kashgar is no secret and it very soon resulted in travel restrictions. The Central Asian Republics followed soon afterwards and now the place to imbibe is across the Indian border, if one can get a visa, that is.

I did not contribute to the economy, however. Raja arrived soon to drive me to Amritsar through a landscape where men did not wear the baggy shalwar of Pakistan. They were dressed either in the narrower pyjama and shorter kurta or Western trousers and mostly chequered shirts, for some reason. And there were colourful Sikh turbans to paint the landscape. Women, other than the occasional bindi, were dressed just the same as women on our side. Seeing my head swivelling around taking in the scenery, Raja, who had been to Pakistan as a peace activist, said it was just the same as the other side. I agreed, but I knew that I was going to compare every little thing with Pakistan.

However, two cultural shocks awaited me as we neared town: girls in jeans and t-shirts zooming about on scooters and pigs rooting in garbage dumps. The latter took a double take because in the initial casual glance they were taken for dogs. As for the girls, they were not really the shock. The surprise was that very few men ogled at them. In fact, the thirteen days I spent in India I squandered all my own ogling chances watching other men's behaviour around random women.

I had done a similar exercise in Afghanistan two years earlier. After years of warfare and ten years of the soul-destroying madness of Taliban misrule in which women were non-existent except as perambulating shrouds, they had suddenly reappeared in all their glamour and beauty. Yet the men in Kabul and Herat, the two cities I visited, did not stare; they simply minded their own business while the newly visible women went by in colourful glory.

Here in our own good land, we molest passing women with our eyes all the time. There appears a well-wrapped shrouded creature with only eyes showing through a narrow slit and all available men leave whatever they are doing to scratch their crotches and ogle. Their heads turn like radar antennas with the passing swaddle of clothing until the poor nondescript thing that could possibly be a woman—if he is not a suicide bomber in disguise—is out of sight. These staring Morlocks would very likely go berserk seeing the bare legs and arms in Amritsar.

Raja, Tahseen had already warned me, had a paunch that could be used as a table—and that was how I recognized him. But that, I realized, was the case with many men in India. It was only towards the end of my Indian travels I realized that in Pakistan we hide our bellies under our voluminous shalwar-kurta suits; in north India most of the men I saw wore Western attire, making their girths apparent. In addition, Indians, it appears, do not suffer from scrotal scabies that Pakistani men are universally afflicted with. This again has much to do with the dresses we respectively wear, for the volume of the shalwar makes it easier than a pair of tight trousers to root about in the crotch.

The first thing Raja asked me was if I was thirsty for a beer. I pointed out that it was too early and the good man told me how his own rather indiscriminate and wanton indulgence had led to liver problems. He said his doctor had advised him to abstain. Having heard tales from Tahseen, I was disappointed.

'So you don't drink anymore?'

'Not really. Even now I don't mind a sip or two.' The phrase he used 'pee-poo laida ey' is richly redolent with typical Punjabi sangfroid and nonchalance.

Dr Parminder Singh, Chairman of the English Department at Guru Nanak Dev University and a friend of Tahseen's from past visits to Pakistan, had kindly made arrangements for me to stay at one of the guest rooms on campus. Raja turned his car into the campus grounds and we drove along lovely tree-shaded avenues with partridges scampering across this way and that. They were apparently never molested and seemed quite at ease. In Pakistan the first thing we would have done is trapped and shot the birds and eaten them to extinction.

After a short meeting with Dr Parminder, as he is known to everyone, we drove to the guest room, dumped my stuff there, and then Raja took me off on the errands he said he had to run. I asked him what he did for a living and his rather enigmatic non-answer left me ever more uninformed. We met Ramesh Yadav whose business card said he was president of the Folklore Research Academy and who, as a champion of Pakistan-India peace, had been across to our side several times. Ramesh said his house was known as Pakistan House because most visitors from our side stayed with him.

We drove to the State Bank of India and on the way Ramesh and Raja had a protracted discussion about a deal involving a graft-seeking politician. I could little make out what the whole affair was about. After another long-drawn-out and, for me, totally abstruse palaver with another gentleman at the bank, we dropped off Ramesh and drove to a blanket factory that Raja said was owned by a 'brother' of his. Another lengthy discussion followed and I learned that this 'brother' had blocked Rs 1.7 lakh in a deal gone awry. Raja was handed a sheaf of photocopied documents. He looked at them cursorily and in a very business-like manner said not to worry; that he'd see what was to be done. We got up to go, but the meeting was not over for it dragged on for another quarter of an hour outside in the street. Clearly, this soft-spoken friend of mine was a real estate fixer as well as general wheeler-dealer.

Raja drove me around to a 'drinking bar', a makeshift bamboo and tarpaulin affair. We were joined by Ramesh and over beers the two discussed yet another problematic transaction. I have to admit that being rather dense regarding financial matters, I could make out nothing of the affair, except of course that some politically important person was at the centre of the chicanery. This was so much like home!

After a hurried lunch at a dhaba next to the bar, the two dropped me at the university and said they had to go off to Ajnala on the border where the Ravi River makes a sharp loop back into Indian territory. Raja, or both of them, had a fishing contract there and they were on their way to apprehend poachers. They said they would have loved to take me along to see the action, but Ajnala being smack on the border was out of bounds for me. As they drove off, I had the feeling these two busybodies lived very crowded and perhaps even somewhat dangerous lives.

When they returned at about seven in the evening, it was in a thickly dust-laden car. The young poacher was found at the river all right, said Raja. But he was not poaching and they had to let him be with just a stern warning to watch his step. We drove to another drinking bar where we were joined by another friend who seemed to be called Chingan. For some curious reason, in Indian Punjab all bars are 'drinking bars' and every store dealing in alcohol is an 'English Wine and Beer

Shop'. A bottle of Royal Stag whisky was ordered. Raja told me that since his doctor's order he had confined himself to two drinks a day. But it was a very serious affair between him and the bottle, with the rest of us contributing our two bits each. After we had polished it off, Raja ordered another half bottle.

'I'm supposed to have just two drinks a day, but every other day I exceed the allocation,' he explained without being asked. I later found out it was not every other day. It was at least twice every day!

Ramesh was fun, but Raja was the star. After the two fed me dinner—they were surprised that I was vegetarian, from a country where people seemed proud of being meat-eaters—and drove me to the university, they said they were calling it a day. But the next morning Raja had another tale to tell. After dropping me off, he had driven to a nearby village famous for its moonshine. Desi, as it is known in the subcontinent, is brewed from various things, mostly the bark of the acacia tree richly flavoured with cinnamon, and fermented in terracotta water pots before being distilled. In Pakistan before the prohibition imposed by Zulfikar Ali Bhutto in 1977, moonshine, even though illegal by law, was a popular rural cottage industry and rarely could a wedding celebration be complete without a liberal supply of it. Himself an avid imbiber, Bhutto instituted prohibition to please the mullahs in order, so he foolishly believed, to garner their support and retain his prime ministership for a second term. The business prospered greatly after Bhutto's folly sent the price of manufactured alcohol through the roof.

TWO

I was on the Shatabdi Express in pre-dawn darkness. It was not yet light when we stopped at Jalandhar railway station. From there, Railway Road leads straight into town and there, about a couple of kilometres from the station, stands the two-storeyed house called Habib Manzil. There, in another life, in a different history, I could well have been living today. That house, of which I had only seen a single photograph taken by a visiting relative in 1985, was the object of this pilgrimage, and like all pilgrimages, mine had a design that I was to follow religiously. Therefore I did not get off at Jalandhar.

The railway buff in me who has ridden trains in Pakistan, not for getting anywhere but for the pure joy of railway journeys, for the thrill of the woof-chug of steam locomotives and the clickety-clack of the big steel wheel on the rails, found myself comparing the Indian railway with what we have at home. The Shatabdi runs the 400 and some kilometres between Amritsar and Delhi in six hours and thirty minutes. And it arrives on the dot. The sound of the train whizzing along the modern track is the same as I have heard in the West, almost like a thin scream because of the high speed at which it runs on perfectly laid tracks.

In Pakistan trains are lumbering slowpokes in which it is almost impossible to manage a cup of tea without spilling even as they crawl along at less than 100 kilometres per hour. The tracks—those few that still operate after most have either been uprooted or simply closed—are antiquated despite claims by authorities that they have been revamped. For many years my favourite train was the Lahore-Rawalpindi rail car that was supposed to cover the 220 kilometres in five-and-a-half hours. In the 1990s, this once great ride was never less than an hour-and-a-half late. I rode it in 2005 when it was a record four hours late. That was the last time I ever used it.

That was not the only train running late, however. In the first decade of the twenty-first century, the Pakistan Railway was a behemoth that was going nowhere except down the tube. With most lines shut down and less than a hundred serviceable locomotives, we had trains running only on four major lines and none of them operated on time. In 2006, travelling from Lahore to Rohri in the middle of the country, I was eight hours behind in a journey of 800 kilometres that normally took about thirteen hours.

On the Shatabdi, looking out to the landscape whizzing past, I found myself wondering why Pakistan could not have a railway like India's. The answer, I already knew. Perdition began with the setting up of the army-run National Logistic Cell (NLC) in 1978 by the deceitful dictator general. The excuse was that Pakistan Railway was slow in haulage and a faster system was needed. Little thought was paid to the fact that after the initial 300 kilometres, haulage by rail is a mere fraction of the cost of road haulage. All the dictator and his cohorts could see were the fat commissions to be accrued from suppliers like Mercedes-Benz, Renault, Fiat and Calabrese—NLC's major suppliers of lorries and rigs. Though commissions on the purchase of locomotives would have been equally lucrative, the dictator had his eyes on the huge income from freight haulage his organization would make over the years. This was the first move to turn the army rentier.

No railway system in the world, no matter how efficient and corruption-free, profits from passenger haulage alone. Freight is *the* earner for a railway and the army's logistic cell slowly bled Pakistan Railway to death. From more than 1,200 functioning railway stations inherited from the British at the time of Partition, there were less than 500 working in the first decade of the twenty-first century. Whereas India laid several thousand kilometres of new track (and revamped all outdated ones) to take high speed trains, Pakistan Railway continued to trundle along in an age warped to the 1940s.

Not only were no new tracks laid, some two dozen branch lines were closed and simply abandoned in the 1980s. Those who lived by the side of the tracks filched the steel and fittings. Disused railway stations were permitted to be annexed as private residences by anyone who felt so inclined. No action was taken when ordinary folk took over railway land to build upon it. In a word, Pakistan Railway was a microcosm of the rest of the country, which had been turned into a free-for-all by the military dictator of sham piety.

India, a vast country with population to match, did the right thing upgrading its railway system. Not only have they revamped old lines, they have also ensured proper working of the system. If a train is to halt two minutes at a station, it more or less does that. In Pakistan, on the other hand, a one-minute halt can drag on to twenty or more minutes. As well as that, there are several thirty-minute halts, even for express trains, on any journey on the main Peshawar-Karachi line. Ask a railway official and he will tell you this is to 'take on water'. As if Pakistan is the only country where trains need water.

At Delhi, I was met by an assistant of Vijay Pratap's. I had been referred to Vijay by my friend Tahseen in Lahore who had attended a training seminar with him back in the early 1980s. The month-long seminar and travels over much of India had made for a lasting friendship and Tahseen had said I was bound to hit it off with him fabulously. Within minutes of our meeting I knew why: Vijay, exactly my age, was an incurable idealist. A hardcore socialist and politically very alive, he was, by his own account, 'a politician looking for a political party'. For a living, Vijay runs an NGO and he had arranged for me to stay in his organization's guest house in Munirka, not far from Jawaharlal Nehru University in south Delhi. It was a first floor flat in a back street overlooking a number of one-room warehouses for various brands of aerated drinks. From the balcony I saw a traffic of very pretty girls with Tibetan features and the guest house attendant told me they all lived in nearby flats. I sat in the balcony watching the men below load their pick-up trucks with cartons of plastic bottles and not give up everything to stare at passing women, many of whom, as I noted with delight, were real lookers.

It was the evening before Holi and from the rooftops children were flinging coloured water balloons on passers-by in the street. There were also groups of teenagers walking about with squirt pumps. So I made myself scarce. Vijay's man who had collected me from the railway station said he could take me either that same evening or on the morrow to see Holi and was taken aback when I bluntly told him I had no desire to see Holi or anything else. I did not tell him that my journey was of a different kind and that I would one day return to see Connaught Place and the ruins of Tughlakabad and everything else that Delhi has on offer. But right now I was on a pilgrimage of sorts.

For me it was a Holi of seclusion in the colour-free safety of the guest room. On the day after the holiday, my friend Ramneek Mohan who taught English in a private college in Rohtak drove over to chaperone me to Irwin Hospital. A few years earlier in a balmy March, Ramneek and a bunch of peace activists had visited Pakistan. Most of the group comprised young people, while Ramneek was about my age. On their last evening in Lahore, they came to our place for dinner and then dossed down in our spare room. Ramneek's family was from our side of Punjab and, speaking of that long ago upheaval, we felt we were kindred souls and a friendship began. We kept in touch by telephone and email and I had informed Ramneek of my planned visit. Earlier when I was still in Amritsar, we had spoken on the phone and he'd insisted on coming over to meet me in Jalandhar to accompany me on my quest for my grandfather's home. I explained that it was a very private mission, almost a pilgrimage, and I wanted to be by myself on it. Now the good man was insistent that we visit Irwin Hospital together.

In 1947, my late uncle Dr Habib ur Rehman had worked here as an intern. One day in early August he received a letter from his sister Tahira, the baby of the family, who was visiting with her older married sister Zubeda in Solan. Things were a bit tense in this quiet sub-alpine town, she wrote, and could he please come up and escort her home to Jalandhar?

The older sister (who was later to be murdered in her home in Rawalpindi) had been living in Solan for the past few months where her husband, Mian Mohammad Sharif, was posted as surveyor with the Survey of India. They had a daughter who was a year old at the time. It was to see them and to get away from the monsoon heat of the plains that Tahira, barely twenty-two, was visiting Solan during her long summer break from college.

Chan took a few days off from his assignment in the surgical ward and rode the trains to Solan. He collected his sister and together they travelled to Jalandhar. When I had first applied for the Indian visa in 1997, there was a brief mention of Partition at home and Chan had remembered the tense air in the railway carriage occupied by men and women of three faiths. Having stayed overnight with the family in Jalandhar, Chan took the train back to Delhi. It was the eighth or ninth day of August 1947. That was the last he was ever to see of his parents, his sisters Jamila—second after my father, who, separated from her police officer husband, was living with her parents—and Tahira, his maternal grandfather and the servant Eidu and his wife Fateh and their five children. This was the journey I wanted to make: from Irwin Hospital to a house in Solan and thence to the home in Railway Road, Jalandhar. This was my private pilgrimage on which I wished to be by myself.

Irwin Hospital, as Chan knew it, no longer exists. The old buildings have been replaced by new, multi-storeyed ones. The dream of walking the corridors where Chan walked more than sixty years ago could not be realized. All that remains from Chan's time is the administrative block with its stubby tower and two short wings. Being a Sunday, the Medical Superintendent was not available and we were told by the two clerks in the office that photography around the admin block was prohibited. I said this was just like home: ask a low-ranking official permission for something and the answer will always be 'No'. The younger of the pair turned on me and snapped, 'We are the same people. So how can you be any different because of the border?'

The poison lay not in the words; it was unconcealed and blatant in the way he spat them out. My fourth day in India and this was the first evidence of cross-religious hostility. Lying in bed that night, all of a sudden I was seized by a terrible uncertainty about the other monuments this pilgrimage had been undertaken to see. Would any of them, the house in Solan and, most of all, the one in Jalandhar, still be there? I had waited a quarter of a century to begin this journey, was I, after all, too late in coming?

I could not return to the hospital the next day because I had still to visit the office of the Divisional Engineer (DEN), Northern Railway. Before Partition, Delhi lay on the North Western Railway and in late 1946 a young man with a wife and year-old daughter had come on promotion from Dharampur on the Kalka-Simla narrow gauge section to take over as DEN. His name was Abdur Rashid and he was my father. In July the following year with things careening madly towards the greatest holocaust ever, he, having opted to live in the new country was transferred to Karachi. Before the end of August, with the fires of communal hatred still raging, he was assigned as DEN Quetta.

It was my father's office I wanted to see in the hope that the incumbency board from those pre-Partition days would still be intact with his name on it. The office I fetched up at was in the unattractive two-storey building adjacent to the New Delhi railway station. Bhopinder Kumar Sharma who sat in the DEN's seat greeted me with great warmth when he heard the reason for my visit. When the incumbency board was all used up, he said with a wry smile, it was painted over and begun anew. History was not preserved as it was at the Lahore Railway Headquarters where I have seen boards with pre-Partition names as well. The current one in Sharma's office went back to 1990 or thereabouts.

Some colleagues of Sharma's walked in. We were introduced, and I was completely taken by the cordiality and fellow-feeling of these good people. It was as if I were family. This was in sharp contrast to the clerk in the admin office at Irwin Hospital. That specimen obviously was an aberration. In Sharma's office, these were human beings from the present who viewed the violence of Partition as sinful madness. Discussions broke out if my father could possibly have held office in the building at Kashmere Gate. Or could it have been in Paharganj? No one was certain, but one thing they knew: there was no incumbency board in any office that went back sixty years. (Back in Lahore, I learned from my mother that my father had worked at the Paharganj office.)

Ramneek who had accompanied me to Irwin Hospital and was now chaperoning me, insisted we visit the ruins of Tughlakabad and the old city. But I did not wish to go anywhere. All that remained to be done was to visit Surindra aunty. Her late husband Prem Nath Sood had gone to the prestigious Thomason College of Civil Engineers at Roorkee with my father. After graduation, my father followed him to the railways a couple of months later and both were posted on the North Western

Railway. Back in 1943–1944 when my father was stationed at Dalbandin in Balochistan, Prem uncle was in Quetta. Both were Assistant Engineers (AENs) and the old friendship flowered. I have a vague memory of Prem uncle visiting us in the Durand Road home in Lahore sometime in the early 1960s.

Partition drove them to different countries upon the same common land and they kept in touch, first by letters and then by telephone. Prem uncle and Surindra aunty were safely in India when the land was divided, but Gyan Nath, Prem uncle's younger brother, was still serving his bank at Quetta where my father was then the DEN. As law and order spiralled out of hand, Gyan Sood gave up his bachelor's residence and came to live with my parents in No. 9, Colvin Road. It was during this time that word, amorphous and uncertain, came across of the terrible carnage in Jalandhar which had possibly engulfed my father's family.

'So that no vindictive thought for Gyan should cross your mother's mind, Bhai Rashid did not tell her that his family in Jalandhar was believed to be no more,' Surindra aunty said. Gyan, whose common bond with my father was a great love for Persian and Urdu poetry, remained with my parents until sometime in November when he was safely expatriated to India.

◆

Mission somewhat accomplished in Delhi, I took the night train to Kalka. The Kalka Mail, originating in Howrah on the west bank of the Hooghly River drew into Delhi station on the dot at five minutes after ten. Not being an express train and yet arriving punctually after a journey of more than 1,400 kilometres was no small miracle, at least as far as I was concerned. The bigger surprise was that the next morning we pulled into Kalka station, the last broad gauge station on the line, in pre-dawn gloaming, again right on time.

Hence onward it is the narrow gauge toy train that runs all the way to Simla via Solan. When Chan went to fetch Tahira phuphi he had taken the train, but averse to waiting a few hours for the train, I took a taxi instead. Surindra aunty, who maintains a summer home in Simla where she annually retreats, had warned me about Solan being grotesquely bloated now and bursting at the seams. It was, I found, more sprawling than Abbottabad.

Rakhila Kahlon, the charming young assistant commissioner, said there was no Survey of India establishment in Solan any more. But she knew there once was and she said she had the right man to trace old properties. A wizened old man (whose name I never asked) walked in with his files held close to his chest and took thirty minutes to come up with the location of the two bungalows that were rented by the Survey of India in the 1940s. They lay to the northeast of the AC's office and, shortly after Partition, one of them was turned into a school. Then in the early 1990s, being private property, they were both pulled down to raise multi-storey hotels or something. He offered to take me to see the new buildings. But I had no interest in them and thanking Kahlon and the man, I came out to walk up and, down the Solan main street.

As I was walking along the footpath past some stores, the side door of a parked lorry suddenly flew open and I had to jump out of its way to avoid being hit. The man about to alight immediately pulled the door back in, and addressing me as 'babu sahib', offered a very profuse and wordy apology. In Pakistan this is never done. No one ever apologizes, especially when the other is a stranger. I have been in hundreds of situations where any decent person would express regret and the only time it ever happened was in Chaman on the Afghan frontier in Balochistan. It was in 1995 and I was walking along a rain-drenched street when a taxi driven by a bearded Pathan came speeding towards me through the water. Fearing a soaking, I squeezed myself as close to the wall as possible. All of a sudden the vehicle braked hard, almost to a crawl. The man stuck his head out and said, 'I'm very sorry, sahib.' I remember thinking at that time how strange it was that the apparently uncouth driver should be sorry even when he had stopped well before he could have splashed me.

◆

Just days after her sister Tahira had left for home with their brother Habib and the ancient land was on the verge of division, Zubeda phuphi and her surveyor husband were alerted late one evening by the roar of an approaching mob. In the distance they could see the flickering light of the faggots borne by the rabble. Aware of the terrible outbreak across the land, they would have been expecting trouble. Quietly leaving the main house, they slipped into the vacant outhouses in the back— my aunt with her infant daughter in one and her husband in the other. Their blood must have all but frozen as they heard several footsteps approaching even as the rest of the mob was ransacking their home.

The door was thrown open and a burning torch held inside

to light up the dark, empty interior of the disused room where my phuphi hid. A voice announced, 'The Muslas have fled', and then the footsteps receded. All the while, Zubeda phuphi remained in the narrow lee behind the door fearing her daughter would yet cry out and give everything away. When the coast was finally clear, leaving his wife and daughter, my uncle clambered over the rear boundary wall and crawled through rank vegetation to make it with some difficulty to the residence of his British superior. The man was apprised of the dreadful fate that very nearly befell my uncle and his family.

And so it came to pass that they were retrieved and eventually made it to Pakistan. Sharif phupha, a man of ruthless honesty and an acid tongue, rose to retire as the last civilian Surveyor General of Pakistan in the early 1980s. Thereafter the army annexed this institution as well. In November 1996, Zubeda phuphi, then seventy-three years old, who had escaped right under attackers' swords in Solan was murdered in her Satellite Town home by her Kashmiri servant. The home where they had lived, the outhouses behind whose timber doors they sheltered from murderous madness had fallen to progress and development. As I paced along the bazaar, I was again overcome by the nagging uncertainty of what I might not find in Jalandhar too.

With time to kill, I walked to Solan railway station for no reason but to watch the narrow gauge diesel-powered trains chugging by. It was early in the morning and March being chilly in Solan, I found the station master and his staff sitting across the tracks from the building sunning themselves. I walked over and told the master that my father had been the AEN on this line back in 1946. Suddenly we were like friends and tea was ordered. The house in Dharampur, my parents' residence in that

Salman Rashid

bygone time, was now a hostel for railway officers attending a training school at that station, the station master said.

We talked railways for a bit and I learned that the narrow gauge section from Kalka to Simla was run by indigenously produced diesel locomotives of the toy gauge after the old steam engines had reached the end of their life. According to him, this change occurred sometime in the early 1980s, perhaps even a little earlier. The locomotive manufacturer was the infallible Tata Motors Limited. The man also told me that the track had been renovated several years ago and could take faster trains.

In Pakistan we could have done the same with the precious Zhob Valley Railway (ZVR) of Balochistan that had, at 2,224 metres above the sea, the highest narrow gauge railway station anywhere. But we abandoned it to the vagaries of nature and thieves. Station buildings on the ZVR have been taken over as private residences and steel tracks removed and sold by crooks who knew that with the British gone the state no longer existed.

The friendliness of the station master and his staff sent my mind back once again to the abrasive clerk in Irwin Hospital.

It took half a day by bus from Solan to Jalandhar. The first part to Chandigarh was by a rickety local bus, the rattle of whose windows still rang in my ears hours after I had disembarked. Chandigarh, an ordered, new-fangled city, is the same sort of inorganic nightmare as Islamabad. As we drove along its long and straight dual-carriageway roads, I resolved to one day return to explore its geography and raison d'être.

The bus depot where the journey from Solan ended was not the same where the journey to Jalandhar would commence; that terminal lay on the other side of town to which I rode an autorickshaw. The air-conditioned bus left at noon and past the order of Chandigarh, we were in countryside that could have been anywhere in Punjab on our side of the border—the only two differences being the t-shirt and jeans-clad girls riding their motor scooters and no one staring, and the 'English Wine and Beer' shops on the main streets of even the dumpiest little village.

We went by a town past a large industrial estate with signs reading Chakwal Group of Industries. Like the many I have seen in Lahore who yearn for and name their businesses after Kanpur, Amritsar or Jalandhar, one rich man has kept alive the memory of a lost homeland by calling his enterprise after it. In a few generations these cross-border titles might disappear as, I believe, Kanpur Leather of Anarkali in Lahore is no more. Until then the anguish of Partition persists.

THREE

Alighting from the bus, I was setting foot for the first time in my life on the soil of my hometown. If my destiny had willed any differently I would have been a Jalandhari instead of a Lahori. In Delhi and Solan everyone spoke Urdu (or Hindi, if you please), now at home it was Punjabi all the way—even with the rickshaw-pullers who were mostly from Bihar or UP. They were mostly Muslims and every single one I quizzed came from an oversized family. They all spoke of upward of a dozen siblings, alcoholic fathers, utter poverty and therefore no education in their families.

A week previously, in Amristar, Dr Parminder Singh had instructed me to call him from Solan to ask about my lodgings at Jalandhar. On the phone he said I was to head for Desh Bhagat Yadgar and ask for a Gurmeet Singh, who would have accommodation ready for me. A large property set in sprawling grounds shaded by beautiful spreading trees, the Yadgar comprises a couple of auditoriums, a hostel of some dozen rooms and a busy kitchen.

The hall commemorates martyrs of the 1857 upheaval—

Mutiny for the British and War of Independence for the people of the subcontinent. Black and white framed images, some of poor resolution, others better, of those heroes and heroines adorn the walls of a ground floor auditorium. There were also a few paintings, presumably of those whose camera image was not available. If I am not wrong, there would be upward of two hundred images in all. And unlike us in Pakistan where we sing only of Islam, the commemoration at Desh Bhagat rests on loyalty to the land. It has nothing to do with one's creed.

Desh Bhagat Yadgar is a non-governmental organization run on donations and is home to jogis (renunciants) of the twentieth century. Like old-time jogis, these men and women have given up everything worldly to keep alive the memory of the martyrs. Gurmeet was one such who administered the organization. So was a clean-shaven Amolak Singh who, having completed his engineering in 1975, did not care to follow the humdrum life of a good job, ease and worldly wealth. Instead, living a rather spartan life off the meagre earnings of his agricultural lands, he travels around with a drama group enacting patriotic Punjabi plays. Amolak hinted that some of his work was not appreciated by the authorities and there had been times when he had to go underground.

After I was settled in a room in a detached wing of the then deserted premises, I returned to the front office where Gurmeet was conferring with three other Sikh gentlemen. He informed the company of the purpose of my journey and the three responded very warmly. Tea was called for and we talked of Partition: only two of the three older men remembered the time; the third, being too young then, knew only what he had heard. Gurmeet and I were of the post-Partition generation.

Someone asked if I knew where my grandparents' home was and I pulled out the photocopy of the only photograph of the exterior of the house that my family had kept.

Taken in 1985 by our mamu Abdul Haq, it shows a two-storey house with shops on the ground floor and stylish windows above a cantilevered overhang on the first. Opposite and across the road from it stands a building with a curving façade and a sign reading 'Lyallpur Sweets'—which, I believed, would make a specific landmark. Other than that, I knew the house was on Railway Road.

'This was Bhagat Singh Chowk,' Gurmeet said, 'and Lyallpur Sweets is no more.' He was not sure if the house I sought would still be there because of the way people were pulling down old properties to raise new multi-storey buildings. Earlier, in Delhi, I had shown the same picture to my friend Ramneek and had mentioned the confectionary shop as a landmark. The hope was that Ramneek, having spent fifteen years of his youth in Jalandhar, would know the place or have friends there who could tell me something about it. Somehow he misunderstood me and instead of the house I sought, he focussed on Lyallpur Sweets thinking my family had something to do with it. Since it had gone out of business many years ago, Ramneek grieved that I had lost what I had come looking for.

◆

Asking the rickshaw-puller to inform me when we turned into Railway Road, I sat in the topless back with the photo in my hand. Back in Lahore, my mother had no idea how far the house was from the railway station, but she had guessed it would be about a 'couple of kilometres'. As we trundled along the road, every passing house seemed to be my grandfather's until we got to Bhagat Singh Chowk.

There it stood across from the chowk, still recognizable from the 1985 photo despite the large signs covering half of the first floor façade. It was still unchanged from that dreadful moment in August 1947 when its owner, Dr Badaruddin, violently passed away from this life. I got off the rickshaw and stood looking at the façade, taking in the detail of the cantilever of the overhang and the fine woodwork of the windows. The mock pilasters separating the windows were worked with flutes and sprang from fountain-shaped devices to rise to capitals that I am at a loss to liken with any style. There were floral and rhomboid shapes on bases and capitals.

The windows had multi-cusped arches in which the spandrels were worked with curvilinear vines. My grandfather must have spent a pretty penny on this woodwork. Above the windows were glass and timber fanlights to permit light into the room even with the windows closed; at the bottom were wrought iron grills. The top floor terrace was hidden behind a cement screen embellished with bracket shapes and stylized esses. In the centre of this was a whitewashed panel under a pediment shape that once bore the words 'Habib Manzil' after my uncle. The name my grandfather had given his home was obliterated by whitewash.

If history had not taken the course it took in August 1947, if the Muslims had not resorted to Direct Action in Bombay and Kolkata in 1946, if Master Tara Singh had not carried out his dreadful promise of a massacre of Muslims in the event of division, if the Muslims of Rawalpindi district had not begun unprovoked attacks on Sikh and Hindu families in March 1947 and if the trains carrying Hindu and Sikh refugees from what was to be Pakistan had not been attacked, Habib Manzil could have been the home where I would have spent part of my life. Standing across the road from Habib Manzil, I almost saw myself looking down from the ornate windows watching the world go by in the street below.

From as far back as I can remember, my father used to say, 'Fools build houses; wise men live in them'. All his life he resisted building a house for himself and his family, preferring, instead, to live in large rented premises. But things turned bad in the late 1960s when he was swindled of a substantial sum of money and went bankrupt. Even in adversity, he repeated that same phrase even as we drifted from smaller to smaller homes. Now, standing across the road from my grandfather's home I knew how Partition had destroyed my father: his father had raised this beautiful edifice in the 1930s and he could only live in it for a decade and a half.

In 1949, stationed at Lahore as Divisional Engineer at the Lahore railway headquarters, my father was allotted a property in Mayo Road outside the railway enclave of Mayo Gardens. Spread over 2,500 square metres, the palatial house was in the last stages of completion when its owner had to migrate across the new border. When my father went to take possession of the property, he found it occupied by a large number of squatters, all fresh refugees from the other side. He came home to say that he did not have the heart to turn those poor souls out. He said—so my mother reported—'I have the means to build, they don't.' Deep inside he may not have wanted to live in this house that some fool had built for himself. Later, when he did have the means, he never acquired any property. And then he went bankrupt. Looking back years later, I feel Partition had made my father self-destructive. It had deprived him of the will to live and prosper. It was as if he no longer cared what came to pass. The loss in Jalandhar that he never spoke of had made him simply give up.

Habib Manzil fronts Railway Road with a narrow lane running down one side. This alley is now called Krishna Street. Across this alley and also looking out on Railway Road was the house of Lala Bheek Chand Sehgal, who was the same age as my grandfather and good friends with him. That house was also still there and I knew this was my passport to the past because Lalaji's family was certain to still be living there. Like my grandfather's home, this too was fronted by shops at street level.

I walked into Krishna Street and paused at the main entrance of Habib Manzil. If the front was ornate, the side of the brick and mortar home was plain but fairly solid looking: my grandfather had made this a home to be lived in by many generations. But I did not enter. I walked on with my notebook in my hand because in it I carried detailed instructions from my mother to get from Habib Manzil to her father's home in Mohalla Panj Pir.

Krishna Street ended about thirty metres behind the home and turned left. From there a short walk in the direction of Chahar Bagh brought me to a small crossing where, so my mother had said, I was to climb an incline, dhiki in Punjabi. In the intervening sixty years, things had changed somewhat. Now there was a greater maze of alleys and more houses. But once on the dhiki, I turned right per instructions and saw the small crossing beyond which stood a house with lanes on three sides. My mother had said to me in Lahore: there was no other house with lanes running down three sides. There was also a marble plate above the main entrance saying 'Munshi Qutubuddin, Naqsha Navees', she had told me. That was my mother's grandfather who had retired as draughtsman in a government department. Because my parents were cousins, he was also my paternal grandmother's father.

But the plaque was no longer there. I backtracked, looking for another house with lanes on three sides. There being no other I came back. As I was looking around, three young women chatting in a lane on one side of the house smiled at me.

'You've come from Pakistan,' said one, more in a manner of statement than query.

'I have,' I said. 'How do you know?'

'Only people who come from Pakistan look at their old homes the way you are looking at this house,' said the one who had spoken before.

There could be no doubt that this was Mian Qutubuddin's home. As the first-born to the only daughter of this home, my father had been delivered by a midwife in one of its rooms in August 1916. Eleven years later, because her father worked away leaving his wife with the family, my mother too was born here in May 1927.

I went around to the front of the house and my knock brought out a man in his late twenties. Upon hearing the purpose of my visit, Sanjeev Malhotra immediately invited me in. With some excitement he announced to his family that I had come from Lahore to see my mother's ancestral home. There were a couple of preschool children, two slender, young women and a rather plump matron who walked with a waddle. One of the younger women was Sanjeev's wife and the other his elder brother Ram Saroop's. The matron was an aunt, the widow of a paternal uncle. The brothers' parents were both dead.

The girls said I simply had to join the family for lunch. But Gurmeet had already fed me a nice vegetarian lunch at Desh Bhagat Yadgar, so we settled for tea. Later, as Sanjeev (pet named Lovely) showed me around, I felt a pang of uncertainty: my mother had said the home was seventeen marlas and this one seemed much too small.

Sanjeev said their home was only about ten marlas. This, then, was not where my mother was born and had spent her early life. Normally I would have bolted at this stage, but something kept me there and as I was being escorted around upstairs, Sanjeev called Ram Saroop and told him about the visitor from Lahore. I was put on the phone with a man who was almost breathless with excitement thinking I was there only for a short while.

'You cannot possibly leave without seeing me,' he said animatedly. 'Please extend your stay in Jalandhar. I'm right now in Ferozepur on business and should be home by nightfall. I must see you. How long will you be in town? Where are you putting up?'

His questions came in quick succession without permitting me to answer them one by one. He even instructed young Sanjeev that I should not be let out of the house. That I be kept and looked after until he got home. On the phone, Ram Saroop told me the house as allotted to his father after Partition was indeed seventeen marlas. Over time they had cut up the house, retained nine marlas and sold the rest.

I did not stay as long as Ram Saroop had wished, but long enough for a lavish tea over which his wife Dipakshi narrated a Partition episode inherited from her grandmother. Married with four little children she and her husband lived in Jhang, a perilously long way west of Radcliffe's line. As a teacher of English in a local government school, the man was much respected. But when the trouble began and goodness dissolved into evil, miscreants shot and killed him as he made his way home from school one day. With three sons and a daughter ranging in age from two to eight—second in line, Dipakshi's father was then only six—the widow was in immense distress when she was taken in by the neighbouring Muslim family. There she and her children remained until she joined a convoy of refugees leaving under escort for India.

Earlier during my visit, Sanjeev Malhotra had asked the matronly aunt to tell me of the visit of the man from Lahore who claimed this was the house of relatives of his. This would be Mamu Haq who had also brought back, in 1985, the only image we have of Habib Manzil. She said he had them tear down a cupboard for, so he claimed, a good deal of treasure was stashed behind it. Nothing turned up, however. Only they had to replace the old timber cupboard with a new one.

A few years earlier, my mother had told me that her father worked in Kuwait during the 1930s where he received his salary in pounds sterling. In the two or three years of his assignment there, he would return periodically with gold coins that his mother, Maan to everyone, would squirrel away in a cavity behind the hearth in the kitchen. Saira by name, she was a matriarch of means for she was known as Mehlan vali Saira— Saira who owns palaces—because of the several properties she owned.

That was where they should be digging, I told the aunt.

But their kitchen was not where the original had stood. After part of the property was sold, they had to build the present kitchen and it was not known what the new owners may or may not have found in the hollow walls when they altered, if they did, the original kitchen.

Later that evening, back at Desh Bhagat Yadgar, I was informed of a visitor asking for me. It was ten o'clock and Ram Saroop who had just returned from Ferozepur was there on his scooter. We sat on one of the benches under a spreading tree and he told me of his family's background. The Malhotras were natives of Pakki Thatti in Lahore. From the roof of their three-storey home, so the elders would say, they could see the setting sun turn the muddy waters of the Ravi into molten gold every evening. There they were a rather well-to-do family with agricultural lands across the river in Sheikhupura district. They had lost all that and received my maternal family's home in compensation.

This is the time in the narrative also to relive what had transpired in this home back in August 1947. Being the home of Mian Qutubuddin, the patriarch of the family, they all gathered there probably on the twelfth day of the month, just when the clamour was very loud. Here were my grandmother Fatima, my two aunts Jamila and Tahira, my mother's grandmother—the matriarch, Maan, and her husband Mian Qutubuddin. Besides, there were also my mother's brother Abdussalam and an older sister, Sakina. My maternal grandfather, a civil engineer, was away at work in Jabalpur. He made Karachi about three months later by boat from Bombay.

Grandfather Badaruddin came over to his in-laws' home briefly. Maan, so we are told, asked him if he had packed for

Salman Rashid

the move. He had not, for he believed nothing untoward was ever likely to befall him. As he was leaving to return to Habib Manzil to see that no miscreants broke in to burgle the place, Maan insisted that he leave Jalandhar with the rest of the family.

For more than thirty years he had served ailing humanity and was well-known in the city. How could those who had regained good health by his ministrations ever think of harming him? How could neighbours, friends and well-wishers turn against each other? Based on what she heard from Sakina khala, my elder sister Rauha tells me he even believed there would be no need to leave hearth and home and go to the new country; that those who wished would go; others would carry on as always. He thought, too, that everyone would be free to travel back and forth across the border as they had always been in united India. He simply did not see families and friends being divided by the line Radcliffe had drawn only two weeks earlier. It was incomprehensible that the truest Iron Curtain would eventually fall along the new border of this ancient land.

And then, should things careen out of control, the good Lala Bheek Chand Sehgal, my grandfather's neighbour and friend of more years than they cared to count, had assured him the safety of his own home. In case there was ever the eventuality of having to leave home, my grandfather felt he could always do it after peace returned.

From members of the maternal side of the family who made it across, we know that at some point amid the growing turmoil grandmother Fatima said she could not bear being away from 'doctor sahib' and left the rest of the family to walk home the way I had come. She being a much loved daughter, Mian Qutubuddin would not be without her, and saying so, followed her to the Railway Road home. Then it was only natural for the sisters Jamila and Tahira to return home as well to be with their parents. No amount of pleading for them to remain in the house on the dhiki could persuade any of them.

From Sakina khala, as passed to me by my sister Noshaba, I know that it was the evening of the twenty-seventh day of the month of the fast. Sakina khala had been at the hearth boiling a pot of milk for the breaking of the fast when she got caught up with the goings on in the courtyard. As the untended milk boiled over and spilled onto the yellow flames, Maan, so it is reported, had very serious misgivings. The boiling over of milk was as evil an omen as evil could be. The family was to suffer an immense loss, she was reported to have wailed repeatedly. Then that part of the family moved to a refugee camp to eventually make their way to Pakistan by train. That was all we knew.

In the decades between the occurrence and the narration, the event seems to have telescoped in Sakina khala's memory. The twenty-seventh of the lunar month coincided with 14 August that year. To my mind, this event of the final farewell would therefore have transpired at least a day before, perhaps even earlier, not on the very day of Partition. However, we do know that shortly afterwards my mother's maternal grandmother Aisha died of natural causes in the refugee camp in Jalandhar. Within days, a cousin of Aisha's also passed away. Both were given hurried burials in the clothes they wore.

FOUR

In 2008, one of the two shops fronting Railway Road dealt in hardware—as it still does. The other housed a maker of tin trunks, pails and sundry items. Returning from the house on the dhiki, I went into Jaswant Singh Harbhajan Singh Hardware and Tool Merchants. A rather busy little establishment, I had to wait a while to catch the eye of the young, dark-haired Sikh behind the counter. When my turn came, I simply said I had no purchase to make and I was there only to chat with him, for he kept shop in my grandfather's property. Rising spontaneously Iqbal Singh came around the counter to embrace me. He ordered his son to vacate the chair for me, asked if I would like tea or Limca and quickly placed an order.

His own family—both parents were then still alive—had migrated from Daska in Sialkot district. We talked for a while before Iqbal returned to his customers and I just sat there looking out at the road. I do not recall how much time passed when he placed his hand on mine resting on the counter.

'Was your grandfather a doctor?' he asked.

I had not said a word about my grandfather's profession.

In fact, because of the rush of customers we had hardly had a chance to speak in any detail. Then, with his brow furrowed with thought, Iqbal Singh said something to set my pulse racing.

'I have heard the whole story of what happened in this house during the Partition riots,' he said.

He had an elderly customer who knew the whole thing for he or someone he knew was there when it all occurred. Iqbal said this customer was in his nineties. This was my first day in Jalandhar and even with my wild and fertile imagination I did not believe the mystery of my family's fate could unravel so fast. However, Iqbal could not recollect who the teller of the tale was.

'A two-year-old child was flung down from the roof,' Iqbal added as an afterthought.

'But that cannot be. We did not have a child of that age in the family.' Iqbal was adamant. A boy child had been thrown to his death.

Telling him to take his time, I went around the corner to look into my grandfather's home. My knock brought a portly woman to the door. Sour-faced and with a bitter tongue, her look was of unconcealed venom when I told her I was from Pakistan. Her countenance turned outright malevolent when she heard this was my grandfather's home and that I wanted to come in to look around.

'Even if you come in and look, you cannot get this property back!' the woman hissed.

'Bibi, I come from a foreign country. The relations between our two lands are far from amicable. There is simply no way I can even attempt to reclaim this property.' I tried vainly to put the woman at ease. We argued back and forth and then, just

Salman Rashid

as she was about to slam the door in my face, I stuck my foot in and pleaded desperately. Something gave. The harshness of her stare softened for a moment and she agreed to let me in. But only for five minutes, she said.

The door opened into a courtyard on the far side of which was a couple of rooms. The picture of my grandfather relaxing in his chair was very likely taken in one corner of this yard. In the back was, I presumed, the store and to the front the men's room where my grandfather entertained his visitors. There were two other rooms that would have been bedrooms but were now stuffed full with old furniture. Above the kitchen a staircase led into a dining room in the mezzanine floor. Another stairway led to the first floor. It was at the top of this flight where my father had posed for the photo, hands in his trouser pockets. Besides some utility rooms, the first floor had three rooms. One in the back, according to my mother, was the one used by my Jamila phuphi. On the side were two more rooms, also bedrooms. The front was taken by the longish room with the finely worked windows that one saw from the street.

Years ago an older relative had told me that our grandfather disapproved of cinema-going while my father was an avid fan. Whenever the fancy took him, he would steal away from the house to watch the matinee show (the second show beginning at 9.30 p.m.). It was said that my father climbed out of an upstairs window to shinny down the electric pole outside. The caper would surely have been pulled from the ornate windows of this room overlooking Railway Road.

From the courtyard below I could hear the woman yelling about my time being up. I quickly scampered up the last flight to the roof. If, as Iqbal insisted, a child had been pitched to his death in the courtyard below, it would have been from this roof. I looked down to the courtyard where the woman stood calling for me to get out. For a moment I thought if anyone needed throwing down from the roof, it was this harridan and no one else.

This was hardly a way to visit my grandfather's home for the first time in my life. Trying to suck up to her, I asked if she and her family were natives of Jalandhar or otherwise. She, being in her early fifties, was born in Jalandhar but her father was from Gujranwala. To this information, she added a few choice barbs about the Muslims having ruined that city. I so ached to tell her that knowing Gujranwala as well as I did, there was no way anyone could further damage that dirty old dump. But with no indication of even a trace of amicability in the shrew, I kept myself from any frivolity. And then she threw me out of my home.

With time to kill while I waited for Iqbal Singh to recall who I should meet, I checked out the store next to his. Ram Lobhaya Gulati, the maker of tin trunks, was in his late sixties and a jovial, garrulous man whose family had also migrated from somewhere near Daska.

'Oye! You are a grandson of Dr Badaruddin!' he exclaimed upon hearing that my grandfather had once owned the property where he did his business. He addressed me with the familiar *tu* as if to underline his or his family's association with my grandfather.

'You just said you were six or seven years old when your family moved to Jalandhar. I find it strange that you should know my grandfather as if he were still alive when you arrived here.' I was perhaps hoping against the vaguest hope that by some miracle he was the man who knew what had become of the family.

'Everyone knew your grandfather in Jalandhar, even refugees like us from Pakistan,' said Ram Lobhaya. 'He had a good name and old Jalandhari people remembered him fondly even after it was all over.'

He sat me down and despite my protestations ordered a Limca to be followed by tea. We talked of Daska and the stories he had heard from the elders. Ram Lobhaya himself had only vague recollections of the old home. He did not remember which part of Daska his family lived in but felt certain that if he were ever to return to his hometown, he would recognize the streets and perhaps even his home.

Across the road was Kailash Sehgal, also in his mid to late sixties and from an old Jalandhar family. He manages a cooking gas agency from a store in the large property he owns. He had noticed me standing before Habib Manzil the day before. The house was so tastefully constructed, he said, that he had rarely seen anyone pass by without looking up at it. A casual glance was one thing, but the way I had stood there and gazed, he knew I was no ordinary passer-by but one with some connection to the house. Having lived in this same area, his family and mine were neighbours and Kailash had heard of my grandfather. But he had no word on the possible fate of the family. However, he pointed me to the store next door saying the elderly Sudarshan Sethi might be of help.

Although an octogenarian, Sethi was still strikingly good-looking. His family home was some way off in another part of town. He did not remember my grandfather's face, but he said he was known as a good and kind doctor. Then he said something that sent a shiver through my spine: 'Doctor Sahib's daughters were victims of a gross inhumanity.' Beyond this one chilling statement Sudarshan Sethi could tell me no more. When I quizzed him, he said not being a resident of Railway Road, he could not be certain of the veracity of what he had heard. But this, he said, was the usual fate of young women from one religious group falling into the hands of men from the other.

Back in Iqbal Singh's hardware store, there was still no recollection of the elderly customer who had known of the fate of Dr Badaruddin's family. Iqbal said the pressures of business did not permit him to dwell on the question of who it was, but when he was home in the evening with a freer mind he was certain to recall. He said I should return to his store in the morning and he would have someone for me to meet.

♦

I was there thirty minutes before Iqbal came around to open shop. He said he remembered who it was and would take me to meet the family as soon as his assistant arrived. We took Krishna Street to a house in a back alley where our knock was answered by a very frail silver-haired old woman. Iqbal had already informed them about my visit and we were straightaway ushered into a living room where an equally frail man was having tea.

But Tilak Raj Suri was not my man. His family had migrated from Rawalpindi in 1947 when he was in his twenties. Back there in the country that was to be Pakistan he and his wife had been politically very active for a united India. Typical of elderly people whose flock has flown away and who have few people to talk to, they saw me as a godsend. The lady was sent away to dig out pre-Partition images showing the two of them carrying placards in processions in their hometowns. Their stories flowed with abundant verbosity. While the man spoke of his politicking in Rawalpindi, his wife, a native of Lahore, told me of the sterling work her father did as an Urdu journalist and writer. And of course, she herself had been a young political activist striving to prevent the cutting up of our ancient land.

Having deposited me in the living room, Iqbal decamped saying he needed to attend to his store. Instantly, I was drowned in a deluge of long-winded narrations that promised not to end any time soon. I was in the wrong place and in a hurry to get on with my quest but here, between the two of them, was not even a gap in the conversation where I could slip a word in about leaving. After nearly an hour with the wonderful Suris holding forth unstoppably, I was finally able to effect an escape.

This was getting nowhere, I told Iqbal back in his store. He seemed disappointed that old Suri was not the one. But never mind, he said, he would surely remember in the next couple of days.

Meanwhile, Ramneek Mohan had arrived the day before from Rohtak and together with Ghanshyam Bhatt, with whom he went to college in Jalandhar, installed himself as supervisor of operations. For starters, we went looking for the family of my grandfather's friend Lala Bheek Chand Sehgal whose daughters Dhanno and Sheila were friends with my aunts. The property had changed hands since that far-off time and neither its present owners nor the shopkeepers in front had ever heard of Bheek Chand. After much quizzing, we were pointed in the direction of a tyre market where a certain person (I forget the name) could possibly have been Bheek Chand's relative. This too turned out to be a blank. This much however we did learn from the tyre-seller: my grandfather's friend had sold his property and moved away to Kolkata in the late 1950s.

Giving up on the Bheek Chand trail, we turned tack. From one elderly gentleman to another we drove in Ghanshyam's car seeking clues to someone with a connection to my grandfather until someone said he knew Gurdial Singh, the maker of musical instruments, to be an old resident of Jalandhar. Surely he would know something. Telling us where to find the man, which was only a short walk away from Bhagat Singh Chowk, he set us off.

Gurdial Singh, in his late seventies, was the typical Lahori: the same loud and infectious laugh, the sociability, the ready wit and the unrestrained ease to crack a risqué joke. His little shop was crowded with stringed instruments, mostly guitars and sitars with a few violins in various stages of construction or repair. But even he could not help me for he had migrated from Lahore to Jalandhar as a young man during the turmoil of Partition. Back in the home city he had lived in Bawa Park near Scotch Corner—a quiet, upper-class suburb in the elbow formed by the canal and Upper Mall.

Gurdial Singh spoke passionately of Lahore, of his youthful years in the city he still loved and yearned to go back to. His feeling and warmth nearly brought tears to my eyes. Since entering India, this was not the first time that I found myself wondering why it all had to occur. In Pakistan I know of dozens of people yearning to return, just once, to a home they or their elders had known in India. And here we have people like Gurdial Singh who cannot forget the home of a past life or Dipakshi, Ram Saroop's wife, who dreams of a time in the future when the border will dissolve to enable ordinary people to travel to the land of their ancestors. The heartache straddles three generations.

Day two in Jalandhar ended with Gurdial Singh. Iqbal was still unable to recall who had told him of the events that took place in Habib Manzil. In the afternoon, Iqbal had taken me home to lunch with his family. Being very staunch Sikhs, the men, Iqbal, his silver-haired father and his two pre-teen sons Kanwal and Preet, and the women, his mother and wife, kept their hair covered. Over a simple vegetarian meal the father spoke softly and slowly of his youth in Daska. I could feel his anguish for the loss of home and his inability to return there before his days came to an end.

Back at Desh Bhagat Yadgar, Gurmeet Singh had worked his magic. Immediately upon arrival, I had told him I wanted to go to Ughi, my ancestral village, and would appreciate if he could put me in touch with someone who lived there. He introduced me to Bakhshish Singh—tall, slim built, good-looking and clean-shaven, I took him to be a Hindu. From the introduction I understood that Bakhshish would be someone who is called a Punjabi *peyara*—loosely Punjabi chauvinist but with a more positive connotation—in Pakistan. He was either part of a theatre group or had come to watch a play and was now on his way home. Bakhshish lived with his family in Baupur, a village contiguous with Ughi. There his father owned a reasonable agricultural spread and the family was quite well off. The man said I should collect an overnight bag and come with him. But the following day, I was meeting with some more people who were likely to be helpful in my quest. I told Bakhshish I could only come the day after that. He had his car and thought the ride would be more comfortable than a bus or a taxi, but when I remained adamant, the good man felt I distrusted him and was afraid of travelling in his company. I had to do a bit of reassuring that it was not on account of any suspicion or fear that I was not going with him, but that I actually was meeting people on the morrow. I took down his contact details and told Bakhshish to expect me by mid-morning on the day after. I said I wanted to see every bit of the village, the old mosque, the graveyard—if it still existed—and the area where my family lived. I also told him I would be particularly keen to meet any pre-Partition family still in the village.

On the third morning, I was again at Iqbal's door even before he or his assistant had arrived. Kailash Sehgal hailed me from across the road and we had tea together. He was concerned that I had not yet met the person who could unravel my history and that my visa would soon run out. Hearing of my proposed visit to Ughi and that I planned to take a taxi, Kailash said I should not bother with that and he would send the autorickshaw that hauled stuff for him. I was free to keep it for as long as I wished. But since I would be staying nearly the whole day with Bakhshish Singh's family, I said it would be better to return the vehicle so that his business was not affected.

◆

'I tell you, I was unable to sleep all night thinking of who it could have been. I have racked and racked my mind and nothing comes to me,' Iqbal Singh began to speak just as he rounded the corner of Krishna Street to find me standing on the threshold of his shop.

He undid the locks and rolled up the shutters to let in the cleaning boy while we stood outside talking. Once again he mentioned the two-year-old boy tossed down from the roof to the courtyard below. There had to be a mistake for we had no child in my grandparents' home, I reiterated. Again Iqbal insisted that was what he had heard.

We went into the store where the dust hung in the still air, each to take his station, Iqbal behind his counter and I on this side. The minutes rolled by until I was hit by a numbing thought: could it be that Iqbal feared I would turn violent were I to meet the man who had been in the mob killing my grandparents? And could it be that he remembered but was not telling me waiting for my visa to run out?

'Bhai Iqbal, if you fear I might lose my head upon seeing the man, please put this worry out of your mind. I am not a violent person and it is very important for me to meet this person and learn the truth,' I tried to reassure Iqbal.

'I think I know what you are about. And I know you do not wish revenge or anything. I tell you I simply do not recall.'

I reminded Iqbal that I had only two more days. On the morrow I would be in the village and the day after, by 3.30 in the afternoon I had to cross the border before they closed business at 4.00.

Leaving Iqbal to mind his store, I went to Aali Mohalla for the second time in an attempt to follow the instructions of my father-in-law to his home. Turning into the street opposite Qasaiyan vali Gali (Butchers' Alley), I once again lost the trail for the locale no longer matched the description I had. It was only on a subsequent visit with my wife Shabnam that we finally did get to the spot where her father's house once stood.

This was in January 2010 when we had befriended journalist Madan Bhardwaj and through him Councillor Kuldip Singh Oberoi that we made some headway. With Shabnam reading out her father's directions from a piece of paper, Kuldip led us into a street crowded with modern structures–the same I had explored two years earlier. As a native of Jalandhar and resident of Naya Bazaar abutting on Aali Mohalla, Kuldip knew his way around and could also tell when most of the old structures had been replaced by the present ones. We hung a left and walked a short way to an empty plot on our left. The debris and pile of old bricks repeated the story so common in our part of the world: the structure had been pulled down. And this was only shortly before our visit. Shabnam was robbed of her chance to be in father's home by someone's desire to pull down the old and raise a modern ugliness.

Before bringing us to this lane, Kuldip sought an elderly Sikh who he thought was an original native of Jalandhar and could be of help. Darshan Singh lived in a lane off Rainak Bazaar. Short of stature, he was in his late sixties with eyes noticeable for their limpidity. The eyes and the tiny smile gave him a look of beatific pleasance. Breathlessly excited to receive visitors from Lahore, he was however no help for his family moved to Jalandhar from across the new border in 1947.

If Shabnam and I were in a hurry to find her father's home, Kuldip was even more charged up. Refusing Darshan Singh's offer of tea and abruptly ending the interview, he ushered us back into Rainak Bazaar. As we were hurrying towards Qasaiyan vali Gali, Madan came up from behind and said the old man wished to speak with me. I turned to look and some way off Darshan Singh was shuffling after us. There was something the matter with his legs for he could not lift up his feet to walk normally. I back-tracked and as we came up to each other he said, 'I too have seen Lahore!'

That was all. He too had seen Lahore.

His eyes glistened and the smile on his face told a dozen stories of a life years before the one in Jalandhar began in 1947. The look in his eyes, the rapture in his smile and the way he had delivered that simple sentence about Lahore was full of emotion. But I was in a hurry to catch up with the others and he with his infirmity could not keep up with me. I mumbled something, shook his hand and walked away. A little way off, I looked back to find Darshan Singh still standing where I had left him, his eyes glistening and the same beatific innocence on his face. He waved to me.

When we were done with Shabnam's business, I told her if there was one thing we needed to do, it was to spend some time with Darshan and his family. There was still time before dinner at Kuldip's home. We told him and Madan we would join them in an hour's time and returned to Darshan Singh's home.

He was on the roof when we rang the bell. His daughter-in-law called out to him that the visitors who were there earlier had returned. He looked over the balcony and with an excited 'Achha, achha!' hurried down the steps. Fearing he might trip because of his infirmity, I told the girl to help him. But in a trice, the man was downstairs, leading us into the sitting room. Seated beside his wife, he elbowed her, 'Nee, they have come back especially to see me!' He repeated himself three or four times before his excitement abated somewhat.

Then the stories flowed. All that he remembered from Lahore was the zoo where he had gone with his father and brothers when he was six or seven. The only memory that stuck was the tank in the aquarium in which a 'frog' repeatedly swam to the surface before subsiding again. But there were stories also of the upheaval of 1947.

Darshan Singh was eight that year. He was born in a village called Klasswala near Pasrur where his family was comfortably well off. His father ran a thriving restaurant in Rawalpindi's Gwalmandi where the family lived in a rented house near the restaurant. In 1944, Darshan joined Standard High School, not very far from Sanatan Dharma High School. He remembers how he daily used to walk back and forth between his home and school. He remembers the streets, the large pipal tree under which he and his mates played marbles, and the teachers who taught him.

Then one day, in a month he does not remember, young Darshan's world exploded in flames—an event whose cause and meaning his young mind failed to fathom. Though his immediate locality was untroubled, from the roof of their home he and his family could see the eerie glow of fires raging in other areas. Soon after his father Varyam Singh announced that they had to leave Rawalpindi and return to the village. Although he could not name the month, I presume this would have been sometime after March 1947. That was when, encouraged by the events of Direct Action by Muslims in Bombay and Calcutta, the first killings and plunder of Hindu and Sikh families began in and around Rawalpindi. The prelude to the mayhem of Partition had begun.

The train brought them to Pasrur from where the family took a tonga to their ancestral home in Klasswala. There they remained for some time. Though he was unable to identify it then, he felt the coldness of fear that raged through the air like a material being. On the tonga ride, he saw people on the move; people carrying tin trunks and jute bags, kitchen things and bedrolls. They carried little children on their shoulders and containers with cooked food as they led cattle and elderly relatives walking, walking, walking ever eastward. But Darshan's father was not one of them. They were going home to Klasswala.

Darshan Singh's memory of the events is telescoped and he does not remember how long they remained in Klasswala. But here, since his family owned a large house, several Hindu and Sikh families of the neighbourhood gathered in their home for safety. Word was that this part of Punjab would soon be Pakistan and that the non-Muslims would have to go across the Ravi to the east.

This made no sense to the young mind of Darshan Singh. Klasswala was home, he had friends here—Muslim, Sikh, and Hindu. There was Chaata, the barber, who lived nearby and whose children sometimes came around to play with Darshan. And there was Khalil, about fifteen years Darshan's senior who lived in the neighbouring haveli. Also there were other Muslim families in the neighbourhood whose names he did not remember, but who had always been good to him and who, on Eid, sent sewaiyaa, vermicelli cooked in milk, for his family.

But they had to leave. The Sardars Satnam Singh and Gurdial Singh, two influential Bajwa zamindars of the village, organized army trucks to transport the Hindu and Sikh families of Klasswala to Pasrur railway station for the journey across the new line drawn by history across the heart of this ancient land. Darshan Singh remembers that when the train arrived at the station it was already crammed with people leaving little room for anyone else to get in. Women, children, and the elderly were stuffed into the crowded cars while the men rode on the roof.

The train was to go southeast from Pasrur through Narowal and Jassar across the magnificent steel spans of the bridge over the Ravi and deposit its manifest of humanity at Dera Baba Nanak. Now, the bridge at Jassar sits wholly in Pakistan but its piers on the left bank of the Ravi tread the border between the new and the old countries that were to hate each other for decades to come. Halting his train just short of the far bank, the locomotive driver being a Muslim refused to go into the country that was killing his co-religionists.

Outside, amid the tall sarkanda grass, in the drizzle of a wet August night lit again and again by flashes of lightning, the people on the train saw an armed host. If young Darshan Singh also felt the terror that coursed through the passengers of the train, he did not talk of it. But it is doubtful that he did for how can an eight-year-old understand that a place that had always been home could suddenly turn into enemy country, its people ready to kill their erstwhile neighbours.

The Bajwas of Klasswala, who were respected and well-known in the area too were on the same train fleeing the home they had known for centuries. The train had stopped, most of it on the bridge with only the last car still on the embankment, while the men outside on either side of the track waited for the refugees to alight. The noise was about killing them in retaliation because Muslims fleeing westward across India had been massacred. For the first time Darshan Singh was truly terrified. I did not ask him, but I imagine he would have clung to a parent and asked if they were all going to die. I wonder how the parent would have consoled his agitated mind.

No one moved. Darshan Singh does not remember how long that situation lasted, but then the Bajwa elders got off. Addressing the gathered mob one of them called out, 'In the name of God, hold your ground. Do not advance on us for we are unarmed. The driver refuses to take this train across the border. Permit us therefore to cross on foot. Do no mischief to anyone of us.'

In that one instant, something went very right. Something inexplicably human took place: the inherent goodness that lives, even if in small measures, in all human beings came to the fore. The gathered crowd armed with guns, clubs, swords and farm implements ready to kill and rape quieted down. Moments slipped by. The only sound to be heard was the pattering of the thickening drizzle on the steel spans and the carriage roofs. At length, the terrified refugees one by one trickled off the train and made their uncertain way in the rain across the bridge to safety on the other side of the Ravi. The men who would have murdered them as compensation for the death of Muslims elsewhere silently watched them leave.

Darshan Singh recalls that once across the Ravi, the entire trainload of people sat down for no one knew where to go in the dark of the rainy night. Day broke and they found the riverbank and surrounding fields littered with hundreds of human corpses—the unfortunate Muslims whose cruel massacre these poor people nearly paid for with their own lives. On the walk to Dera Baba Nanak and beyond to Batala, Darshan Singh saw the country similarly littered with the dead—the tragic harvest of Partition.

Sixty-two years and four months went by. Darshan Singh finished his education, went to work, retired and grew old but the memory of the home in Klasswala, the school in Rawalpindi's Gwalmandi and the harrowing journey in August 1947 did not leave his mind. Surely, he would have preserved those memories by telling his stories to his children, but I do not know if he had ever met a Pakistani to ask of the land that he was forced to abandon as a child.

I asked him what he thought was that kept the Muslims from turning on them at the bridge. 'The Parmatma dwells in the soul of all humans. There He kept those people from doing evil.'

'But then you saw hundreds of dead on the other side of the Ravi. What of them?' I asked.

'It was a crime against humanity and the Parmatma. Those who killed the Muslims tried to kill God who dwells in our souls.'

Within a fortnight of my meeting with Darshan Singh, I was in Klasswala to see if I could find his home and possibly meet the children of Chaata the barber and of Khalil, the neighbour. I found one old haveli with Gurmukhi lettering on the facade which said 'Fakir's Residence'. It did not bear, as Darshan had said, the name of his father Varyam Singh. Khalil was forgotten and no one had heard of Chaata the barber. I suspect in the disorder of Partition the barber apportioned to himself abandoned properties and, as is the known norm, duly discarded his 'low caste' and converted to Syed.

But I did meet Abdus Sattar in Klasswala, one of the older men who I quizzed about Khalil and Chaata. He was, however, not a native. His family had migrated from Ugala village in Ambala district. As a three-year-old at that time he did not remember anything of the turmoil save what he had been told by his elders. I asked him if his family had been in any peril at any time during the long journey across the rain-sodden Punjab plains.

He spoke of the same goodness of the soul that had overcome the mob waiting to do in Darshan Singh and his fellow travellers. His parents had told him that in that time of heightened hatred and madness their Hindu and Sikh neighbours and friends came forward with unflinching courage to stand by them. Many offered Sattar's family refuge in their own homes while they waited out the insanity. Once it was over, they were told, they could return home and continue to live as they always had.

But other forces were at work and Abdus Sattar and his family were moved to a camp and then to the railway station. Until they were safely on the train, their neighbours who did not have to leave because they were not Muslims, remained by their sides to see that no harm befell them. This called for true grit for it is known that when bloodthirsty mobs descended upon massed refugees, only military escorts could drive them away. Ordinary people defending their erstwhile neighbours were killed the same as those they defended.

That goodness of the soul among one set of people of one religion that preserved the family of Abdus Sattar in Ambala was no different from that which kept Darshan Singh and his fellows from harm on Jassar bridge. Surely if things had only taken just a slightly different turn, this goodness would have prevailed across the land. Then this, the greatest human transmigration accompanied by dreadful bloodshed, would not have happened.

◆

But on that first visit, as I was hanging about the Aali Mohalla mosque, three young men spotting me as a Pakistani came around to talk. They wanted to know how we were different from each other.

'We're just the same,' I said. 'Only in Pakistan we ogle women so hard our eyes pop out of their sockets.'

This elicited a burst of laughter from the trio. There is no way to translate from Punjabi the response of one of the men, but roughly, it would mean that in India they too did not mind an ogle or two.

By evening Iqbal Singh's memory still drew a blank and I had the sinking feeling that despite being so near I was yet too far from my objective. I may after all be right that Iqbal, fearful of my reaction, was holding the name of the person from me. If he did not come forth within the next two days, it would be too late and I would be gone. The way things have always been between our two countries, I was doubtful I would get a visa again in a hurry.

FOUR

The auto-rickshaw man sent by Kailash Sehgal was at Desh Bhagat Yadgar at eight in the morning. We drove through the traffic and were soon out in the country headed south. Somewhere in the vicinity of Lambra, we drove by a pipal tree smack in the middle of the road with the traffic passing it on either side. For a Pakistani this was a gross aberration. Here trees are the first victims of any 'development project'. I have images of beautiful trees that no longer exist because a road passing nearby could not be given a slight bend to save them. I know also of an upstart building his home with a bathroom tile façade and destroying eight magnificent trees outside so that the ugly monstrosity could be seen by passers-by. He was not alone. The first thing anyone destroys outside their home is the tree native to the land.

Our district administration bureaucrats routinely destroy hundreds of years old banyan trees of huge bio-masses that sequester tons of carbon and replace them with date palm or shrubbery. Infatuated with imported species and labelling indigenous ones as paindu (uncool), these philistines with pretences as great as their achievements are insignificant, are busily transforming the Pakistani landscape into a green desert. As our cities encroach upon forest and farmland, trees are being slaughtered wholesale. The replacements are dwarf species and, of late, the wretched conocarpus because it 'grows fast'. One wonders why the Pakistani nation is in such a hurry to get to a green hell.

On a later visit in 2010, with Bakhshish driving Shabnam and me to the village, I jokingly asked why they needed a tree in the middle of the road and suggested it be axed. Bakhshish was aghast. 'Bhaiji, you might get away killing a man, but never even talk of destroying a tree,' the man said with a seriousness that surprised me.

Partition and the drawing of one imaginary line had altered the way how minds of culturally identical humans on either side worked. In India they still value trees that our ancestors had worshipped eight thousand years ago in the cities of the Indus Valley. In Pakistan we think nothing of destroying them.

I do not recall how long the roughly 30 kilometre drive lasted, but it was still quite early when I arrived. Sardar Saudagar Singh, Bakhshish's father and patriarch of the family, wore a white pyjama and shirt with an indigo turban. His luxurious grey whiskers hid the ruggedness of his face, still handsome in old age. He spoke softly in an unhurried manner. He said he was a Kamboh of the sub-caste Josan. I had come home to a kinsman for we Arains are converts from among the Kambohs.

Muslim Arains have over time invented what I call an illegitimate father for themselves to show that they are 'original' Muslims—whatever that means. This specious ancestor they know as Saleem Al Raee. A spurious history of the Arains,

Tarikh e Araian, (History of the Arains) written by a semi-literate person, Asghar Ali Chaudhri, tells us that this ancestor, a heroic general in the army of the invading Arabs, came to Sindh in the early eighth century. One wonders why we all descend from heroic mythical figures. Why no one claims to be a tanner's or a potter's child. The author of that brainless history, of course, gives no reference and leaves the reader wondering from where he gets this name, for the two most authentic histories of the Arab invasion do not contain any such name for a general or even for a common soldier.* Neither does any other history until the 1930s when the name is miraculously revealed to the author of the spurious history.

But this mental sickness of claiming Arab origin is not specific to the Arains. There are no Muslims in Pakistan who do not believe in true Arab blood for themselves. Even thoroughbred Rajputs, Jats and Gujjars, all Indo-Aryan peoples, sing of some fictitious Arab ancestor, a valorous general to boot, who descended upon the subcontinent with the army of Mohammad bin Qasim. So pervasive is this insanity that it begins to seem that until the coming of the Arabs, India was a land inhabited only by wild beasts.

With DNA profiling by laboratories in the West now within reach of anyone, I know of a few claimants of Arab origin who have, much to their distress, discovered the truth. One of them, a military officer-turned-civil servant, once a very vocal

---

*The two histories being *Futuhul Baladan* (Conquest of Cities) of Ahmed Al-Biladhuri and *Chachnama*. The latter based on a now lost eighth-century Arabic manuscript authored by a cousin of Mohammad bin Qasim who served in the imperial army, survives as a thirteenth-century Persian translation by Ali bin Hamid Kufi.

champion of Arab ancestry for the Arains, now hides his face in shame. Poorly educated and raised on religious ideology-based mendacity, we have learned not to be liberated by truth, but mortified by it. As for myself, I was never in any doubt, for the study of history shone the truth upon me thirty years ago. It set me free and instilled in my spirit immense pride in my Indian origin.

Interestingly, this silly eagerness to claim Arab ancestry goes back to the sixteenth century: Abu'l Fazl, official chronicler of the court of Mughal emperor Akbar the Great and one of his Nine Jewels, took a derisive swipe at it. We do not know if the Arains too had embraced it at that early date. However, in the latter years of the nineteenth century when Ibbetson, Maclagan and Rose were compiling their *Glossary of the Tribes and Castes of the Punjab and North-West Frontier Province*, the Arains of Jalandhar had another story to tell.

They were descendants of Rai Jaj, grandson of Loh, the founder of Lahore, so the researchers were informed. This would make them descendants of Lord Rama. It was also recorded that they converted in the twelfth century and migrated to the Jalandhar doab about three hundred years later. Beyond that there was no information. In the late nineteenth century, innocence was not yet lost and the foolishness to be branded Arab had not fully taken over. But with subcontinental Muslims of every hue tripping over each other to claim a bogus ancestry for themselves, the Arains also quickly caught on and by about 1930 the trend was well established.

In their haste to prove themselves 'original' Muslims the Arains are commonly known to boast that there is no non-Muslim Arain. They conveniently forget that Muslim Kambohs also claim to be true Arains and that this section of the caste consists of non-Muslims as well. They also disregard the fact that it is generally believed that Arains and Kambohs share a common ancestry.

The question of where the title of Arain originates is variously answered by pseudo-historians among the clan. While most say it is an Indianized version of Al-Raee, the surname of their fictitious ancestor, others believe it a corruption of Aryan. In this latter case, they fail to see the irony of claiming, simultaneously, Aryan *and* Arab lineage. But then, I suppose, it is not without reason that we are not celebrated for being logical in such things.

I believe Arain is a corruption from overuse of a now forgotten word. I believe when the first Kambohs converted, they were labelled under that now unknown title. At some point, as conversion speeded up, the distinction between Kamboh and Arain dissolved. But when it came time to declare themselves 'original' Muslims, the Arains began to disparage the Kambohs— even though they shared sub-caste names with them—as the untouchables among their caste only because some Kambohs continued to adhere to the ancient creed.

Even as they vociferously claimed Arab descent, the Arains also conveniently forgot that some of their sub-caste names like Ramday, Ramay and Ramkay—to name just three—connect them with the god whose descendants they had once claimed to be. Moreover, their shared caste names with Kambohs, Rajputs and Jats show them to be a true Indian race.

In 1995, during a discussion about the family and their days in Jalandhar, I saw how deep-seated was the desire to forget our Indian-ness and expunge the pre-Islamic past when Chan went so far as to stress there was no need to remember one's ancestry. Besides being an attempt to forget the kafir past, this may also have been another futile attempt to push away the terrible memory of the family lost in Jalandhar.

We do know that by the middle of the seventeenth century there was a Muslim Arain community famous for their skill as gardeners. As Shalimar Garden of Lahore neared completion, Shah Jahan relocated a number of Arain families from the east to a place outside the city of Lahore that is still known as Baghbanpura—Gardeners' Town. Their horticultural skills and diligence made Shalimar a right royal delight. With time, the descendents of this assiduous lot rose in status and by the late nineteenth century were a much respected part of Lahore society. Some of them even being knighted by the Raj. Today the Arains of Baghbanpura are among the better off families of the city, the real keepers of old money against a deluge of nouveau riche enriched by plunder beginning in 1947 and on going. This latter class now plagues the sorry Pakistani social landscape.

But Arains were not just gardeners in the seventeenth century. The writer of the *Shah Jahan Nama*, the official history of the fifth Mughal king, was one Saleh Kamboh Lahori. An able scribe, he was also keeper of the royal library while his father Zafar Khan held high office in the court of Shah Jahan. And, before that, we also know of Shahbaz Kamboh, a nau hazari—commander of nine thousand—a general in Akbar's army who distinguished himself in battles in Bengal.

To Saudagar Singh I said that as an Arain I had come home to a kinsman from a distant past. For the first time his serious mien broke into a rugged smile.

Saudagar Singh was born in March 1938 in a village a couple of kilometres outside Shahkot town (Lyallpur district) unimaginatively named 60 RB (after Rakh Branch Canal) by British colonial officers. So was his older brother; but the eldest who, had he lived, would have been in his mid-eighties in 2008, had been born in the ancestral village of Nizampur outside Amritsar. The Sandal Bar, sandwiched between the Ravi and the Chenab, south and westward of Gujranwala was largely forest and desert until 1892. That year the weir was thrown across the Chenab at Khanki and the Lower Chenab Canal swept southward to transform desert and scrubland. Thousands of acres of virgin land, newly irrigated by alluvium-rich river water, became available in the new district of Lyallpur where the government offered large acreages of canal-irrigated land to farming families from the doabas of Amritsar, Jalandhar and Ludhiana. The land came gratis and was incentive enough to begin a small westward exodus of Hindus, Muslims and Sikhs.

From his elders, Saudagar Singh knew of the migration of several Kamboh families of their village Nizampur. By and by, word came that holders of small agricultural plots of the past were now prosperous landlords in the Sandal Bar. Sometime in the mid-1920s, Saudagar Singh's father sold his property in Nizampur and moved west to begin a new life. Like all other pioneers, he too put his back to the yoke and the virgin land spewed gold. When the troubles of Partition began, the family one day abandoned fifty acres of prime canal-irrigated farmland rich with standing crops and fled.

The memory of the nine year-old reinforced by the family's repeated references to the events of that fateful August holds visions of Sikhs from surrounding areas congregating in their village for safety. The air was heavy with fear that left its metallic taste in the back of the mouth as they loaded bullock carts with items of household use, clothing and food. En masse they went to the neighbouring village of 61 RB peopled by affluent zamindars, also Sikhs of the Bawa sub-caste of Jats.

Though it was known that Lyallpur and their village was well within the new country of Pakistan, Saudagar Singh recalls a degree of uncertainty for after just one night under the open sky in 61 RB, the families of 60 RB returned to their own homes. But the next day a rumour floated that Muslims were preparing to attack Sikh villages to plunder and kill. Assembling again in the Bawa village, the drivers of the cart convoys now turned their faces eastward and did not pause to reconsider the idea of staying. All that had been built over years of hard labour was abandoned. Saudagar Singh for his childish years may not have felt it, but the agony of leaving all behind would surely have added, within days, furrows to his father's ageing brow.

Fear stalked the caravan as the carts creaked southward to Jaranwala at their excruciatingly slow pace. But nothing untoward occurred. Saudagar Singh does not know who chose the route, but they were heading for Kasur to make Khem Karan across the new border. He does remember riding atop the stack of goods on the cart while his father and two older brothers strode alongside. At a village he remembers as Lauka, a military convoy with Gurkha soldiers arrived for their protection. And so they made it across safely.

Saudagar Singh's family was fortunate they had a home and relatives in Nizampur where the maternal side of the family still lived and where they could begin to reorder their devastated lives. By and by, the family was allotted land in Batala district in lieu of the loss of 60 RB. But in 1952, this allotment was cancelled and a fresh one was made in village Baupur. When

Salman Rashid

they arrived here, the village was deserted, recalls Saudagar Singh. All that stood was one partially burnt out house and a badly damaged mosque. A Muslim shrine next to the graveyard was intact. The rest was rubble.

Inured by centuries of marauding incursions by plunderers of every hue coming down after reducing Afghanistan, the Punjabi peasant has learned never to give up. If there is one virtue he, regardless of his creed or caste, can truly be celebrated for, it is the ability to toil unremittingly again and again and again. From the small allotment against the fifty acres lost in Lyallpur, the Josans raised a small empire and today Sardar Saudagar Singh is no mean zamindar of Baupur.

Too young at that time to actually feel its uncertainty, Saudagar Singh remembers the desperation of the years immediately after Partition. The uprooting from the homestead in Batala that his father struggled to establish and the forced move to Baupur told heavily on him.

'Not fully twenty years earlier he had left a small acreage and a very old home near Amritsar of his own will to become a landowner in village 60 RB. Partition reduced him to penury and there seemed no future for us,' said Saudagar Singh.

He referred to Partition as Year of the Perdition (Ujaday da Saal). Whenever in the course of our conversation he referred to it, he said 'when ruin fell upon the land'. This was in sharp contrast to what I have heard in Pakistani Punjab. Here the upheaval has always been referred to as Year of the Plunder (Loti da Saal) sometimes even with a degree of glee attached to the phrase. The same people, speakers of a common language who practice the same culture, were divided in outlook only because in west Punjab there was much owned by rich Sikh and Hindu families for Muslims to despoil. The non-Muslims who fled eastward were ruined. Muslims, native to this side, and those who came from across the new border, looted or appropriated for themselves untended properties to enrich themselves as their generations had never been before.

Saudagar Singh spoke of the land he owns as the property of Arains who had left during the Year of the Perdition. On a subsequent visit in January 2010, he introduced me to Harbhajan Singh Hundal who lived nearby. The man invited Shabnam and me to his home saying the 'owners' of his house also lived in Lahore. Sixty-three years had gone by yet Harbhajan Singh could not but acknowledge the real owners of his property. In Lahore I know of one rich property in Model Town whose original Sikh owners visiting from India were denied entry by the lawyer who had acquired it after Partition.

Just the drawing of Radcliffe's line had had such profound effects on the minds of Punjabis living on either side. For us on this side, 1947 was truly the Year of the Plunder.

◆

In the day and a half since our meeting in Jalandhar, young Bakhshish had been busy locating members of the only Hindu family from pre-Partition Arain Muslim majority Ughi and still living there. Born in 1924, Pundit Fakir Chand Sangar remembered Dr Badaruddin very well. He was doing his matriculation from the high school at Nakodar when my grandfather served the hospital there as civil surgeon. He recalled that doctor sahib wore light-coloured suits and pastel, patterned neckties to work; and knew every single person, young and old, in Ughi by name. Anyone from the village visiting him either at Nakodar or in Jalandhar was greeted and entertained equally. Though there were older gentlemen in the village, my grandfather had the most influence in every matter, he said.

My grandfather was a very humane person, as described by Fakir Chand. He never differentiated between followers of various creeds. Even after his retirement in 1945, when he kept clinic in the same building as Quomi Press in Railway Road, Jalandhar, he was known for his open-minded non-parochial consideration towards all patients, he said.

The doctor's ancestral home, said the Pundit, was in the northwest quarter of Ughi known as Lamyaan di Patti—Precinct of the Tall Ones. Though two of my father's cousins, being well over six feet, were exceptions, we are not a remarkably tall clan. I found the name striking and felt it went a long way back in history when one part of the clan, or perhaps even one extraordinary individual, was noted for his height. Those who may have descended from that person, even today retain their tall stature.

Today Lamyaan di Patti is home to Dalit Balmiki Hindus. Even in 2010, at the time of my last visit, those dusty alleys were bordered by ruined and abandoned houses. There was also a tiny roofless mosque the dust of whose floor would surely have once nestled in the furrows of my grandfather's brow. Nearby, a huge pipal shaded the homes and beyond the houses stretched fields once tilled by those whose blood I carry in my veins.

It was 1942 or the year after, when Fakir Chand attended the Nakodar high school and my grandfather minded the hospital.

'I being from his village, doctor sahib was very fond of me and always addressed me as Pundit,' he said. Appreciative of his ability to write the Persian script in a very fine hand, my grandfather had instructed his staff to have their registers filled in by Fakir Chand. Every afternoon the youngster would come around after school to work and be paid a small honorarium for his labour.

One summer afternoon, a Sikh came to the hospital in great pain. A honeybee was lodged in his ear. Fakir Chand said my grandfather had a post-lunch siesta every day and the staff was not permitted to rouse him. This was so true because the afternoon nap was like religious injunction in our family which we, as we grew up, considered a sickness.

Fakir Chand said the patient was a paternal uncle of the same Swaran Singh who eventually rose to be a foreign minister of India. Nevertheless, the staff under strict instructions against doing so was terrified of rousing my grandfather. In view of his close relationship with the doctor, the unpleasant task devolved upon the Pundit.

'Upon seeing me at the door doctor sahib said, as always, "Haan, Pundit",' recalled the man.

Hearing of the suffering Sikh, my grandfather told him to have the staff ready while he changed. After the man was ministered to, the staff was dismissed and as everyone was leaving, my grandfather told Fakir Chand to stay. What he then said astonished the young man for he had never known him to be like that. Indeed, six decades later, even I was surprised for we had always been told of him as a totally unbiased person.

'Look here, Pundit,' my grandfather is reported to have said, 'you can wake me for anyone, Muslim or Hindu, regardless of where they come from. But never bother me for these Khalsas.' The severity of the doctor's tone took Pundit Fakir Chand by surprise. Fakir Chand said something was happening in those years, something that his young mind could not grasp. Why, even a man like my grandfather was changing. 'He lost his step,' observed the man. Sometime later another awkward event occurred. Never before were the Arains either of Ughi or nearby villages known to have slaughtered a cow for Eid. But in 1944 or the year after, my grandfather said a cow would be publicly butchered on the occasion. Pursuant to the scheme, he even got the necessary license from the district administration.

In the run up to Partition, emotions were already strained and as the day of the sacrifice drew nearer and word got around, Hindus of the area became restive. Word was that Hindus and Sikhs were preparing to block the ritual physically and were ready to use force if necessary. There was every likelihood of blood being spilled—and it was not going to be that of a cow alone. A couple of days before the event, the deputy commissioner and superintendent of police arrived with a force from Jalandhar. According to Fakir Chand extensive parleys were held between Muslims led by my grandfather on one side and Hindus and Sikhs under the leadership of their elders on the other. With the deputy commissioner presiding, it eventually boiled down to a cancellation of my grandfather's permit to kill the cow. Thereafter, a moratorium was placed on bovine sacrifice for the future, said Fakir Chand.

'Doctor sahib had joined the Muslim League. It wrought evil in the mind of such a decent human being as him. I don't understand why that had to happen,' said Pundit Fakir Chand bleakly.

According to him that was the very cause of the tragic slaying in Jalandhar of a man as pious and upright as him. In

Ughi, he said, only one person, Ghulam Mohammad by name, lost his life. All others were safely expatriated across the border. Nor too was there any arson or plunder in the village.

For me my grandfather's attempt to sacrifice a cow was astonishing. As we grew up in Lahore, beef was taboo in our home. My father, a great meat-eater, abhorred beef as food. It was considered somehow inferior to mutton, fit only for the poor. In the 1970s, whenever I was home from the army, my brother Imran and our cousin Shahid would organize barbecue parties on the terrace. The fare was vodka (secretly, for no one drank in our family) and beef kebabs. My father would not even come out on the terrace while the barbecue was in progress. But from time to time we would hear his rant about beef never having entered the home of our ancestors and how shamelessly we were now gorging ourselves on a forbidden food.

We did not understand it then; I do now. This was not the aversion that a Muslim would have for, say, pork. For countless years as Hindus, our ancestors had staunchly abstained from beef until even after conversion they were revolted by the idea of consuming it. We do not know when the Kamboh clan split into Muslim Arains, but six generations before me we have one Hafiz Dargahi beyond whom there is no record. I have a niggling feeling that the good Hafiz's father was a Hindu, or perhaps a Sikh. Having given up the old religion, and overcome with the unrestrained zeal of the convert, Dargahi memorized the Quran to become a Hafiz. Family lore has it that he and his son Mian Eena were both much respected scholars of Islam. Of the latter it is also said that he was Maharaja Ranjit Singh's son Kharak's Persian tutor. But there is no documentary proof in favour of this assertion and I look upon it as a somewhat clumsy attempt to arrogate greatness for a family of poor farmers.

With the old faith fresh out of the soul and the new trend of asserting Arab ancestry with the claim to being 'original' Muslims upon them, the new converts strove with great passion to forget the kafir past. While the old ancestors were forced to be forgotten within three or four generations, veneration for the cow never left their souls. Only now they had taught themselves to pretend it was rather a revulsion for its flesh.

While there are many Arains who do use their ancient family or sub-caste names, the descendents of Hafiz Dargahi were especially keen to erase the heathen past which may be because they were late arrivals into the fold of Islam. None from the Hafiz's progeny know which sub-caste they belong to. The only name used in our family is Mian which is neither here nor there for it is simply a title of respect. Mian is also popular among the Rajputs of Rajasthan and was once the common form of address among Muslims for theologians and teachers.

And there in the mid-1940s was my grandfather who, if I am to go by reports, could not have thought of such a thing only a few years earlier, was now bent on sacrificing a cow. A most peculiar sacrifice this would have been for a man who abhorred beef all his life.

FIVE

Done with Pundit Fakir Chand, Bakhshish and I returned home to lunch with his father. We had barely started when my phone rang. It was Iqbal Singh from Jalandhar. He had, after all, recalled who it was and had spoken to the gentleman. And the man wanted to see me.

My appetite vanished. I breathlessly narrated the whole story of how, on the very first day, Iqbal had tantalized me with this little bit of information about what had transpired in my grandfather's house only to give rise to the impression that he feared my reaction upon meeting the man who knew the story. I found it difficult to hold myself down. Sardar Saudagar Singh smiled at my state and encouraged me to eat my fill before I left his home. The plan had earlier been for Bakhshish to drive me to the Ughi taxi stand where I would hire a ride back to Jalandhar. But now my host instructed his son to take me all the way back to Railway Road.

But before I left Ughi I had two things to do. One, we drove back to Lamyaan di Patti for me to collect a handful of dust. On my return to Lahore, I would sprinkle some of it on the graves of my father and Chan. The rest I keep in my study in a marble container. If I die of natural causes instead of vaporizing in a terrorist attack and have a decent burial, I would rather like my shroud to first of all be stained by the dust of Ughi. That dust is sacrosanct for it bears the scent of those who went before me and whose blood courses in my veins.

I also wanted to check out the old graveyard in the hope of finding a known name on the gravestones. Sardar Saudagar Singh said he remembered a spreading burial ground next to the Muslim shrine. But decades ago, the graves were bulldozed and a grain market built over the bones of my ancestors.

Though there remained a handful of Muslim graves still, there was just one gravestone almost abutting on the wall of the Muslim shrine. It read, 'Allah di Jheeri Mastani' who died on the fourth day of the month of the fast in the Hijri year 1357. This corresponds with 28 October 1938. There was no year of birth. From 'Mastani' it appeared she was mentally challenged in some way. Back in Pakistan there was no one left to tell me who this woman was.*

We also looked into the shrine. Brought up in a staunch Hanafi Sunni household, I had learned to disparage shrine worship as heresy. Seeing the Sikh keepers reverently fanning the grave in the afternoon heat, I said something about the dead man very likely being a fraudster and how could the Sikhs be so taken by a Muslim burial as to be whisking away its flies.

---

*On the authority of Mushtaq Soofi, noted Punjabi intellectual, Jheeri denotes a woman who keeps a tandoor to roast grain. Could it be that this woman, somewhat intellectually challenged, did this service in Ughi?

Bakhshish had to do a job dragging me out of the ensuing argument.

What surprised me was that they were keeping a Muslim tomb complete with its tombstone and Arabic inscriptions. In Pakistan, tomb-worshippers revere only those non-Muslim burials that have posthumously been converted to Islam. And there are many of this kind across the country. All other known Hindu shrines have, at best, been neglected and at worst vandalized. That having been said, it must be granted that the government did begin an effort at restoring some of the more important shrines. Despite the stringent visa regime, temples like Ketas Raj near Chakwal and Sri Mata Hinglaj on the Makran coast of Balochistan, two of the holiest Hindu shrines in Pakistan, are now active pilgrimage sites. For some reason the several Sikh shrines of Punjab have fared rather well. Sites like Panja Sahib of Hasan Abdal, the birthplace of Guru Nanak Dev at Nankana and Gurdwara Kartarpur, the site of his death near Narowal, together with minor shrines have all been well looked after and annual pilgrimage permitted to them.

◆

I got off in front of Kailash Sehgal's gas agency and even as I was saying farewell to Bakhshish, I heard Kailash say, 'Rashid sahib, please come here!' My first thought was that he might have something new to tell me about my grandparents' last days, but the sharpness of tone caught me by surprise. I climbed the steps into his store as he got up to come around the counter.

'Why did you do this?' he asked, clearly miffed.

'Why did I do what?' I countered as he reached forward

and quickly stuffed something into my breast pocket.

It was four hundred rupees.

'What is this for?' I was at a complete loss to understand what was going on.

'You were not supposed to pay the autorickshaw for the ride to Ughi!' he said. Now he sounded more hurt than upset. In the morning, when I left the rickshaw at the Josan residence, I asked the man what I owed him and paid the named price. Now I felt embarrassed. Embarrassed and thankful to a good man who was doing this because even if he himself did not know them, his elders had known my family in another age.

Iqbal Singh was waiting. The minute he saw me cross the street, he got on the phone. And five minutes later Mohinder Pratap Sehgal walked into the store. A little shorter than me, stocky and bespectacled, he talked fast. After the initial introduction, very strangely I went into a trance-like state. It was as if I was watching a movie at fast-forward speed. As he spoke, I took out my voice recorder and held it out. It was only later that evening in the solitude of my room in Desh Bhagat Yadgar that I came to grasp every word he had spoken.

'Look here, I have first of all to ask forgiveness for it was my father's mistake,' Mohinder Pratap began and I simply did not register what he said.

As he spoke I thought he was referring not to his father but to someone in the mob for he referred to him as bevakoof (foolish) and tung dil (mean). It was he, said Mohinder Pratap of his father, who, because he ran after Eidu, gave away my grandparents' hiding place.

'Come, let me show you how it all happened,' taking me by the hand he led me out of Iqbal's store.

I had not mentioned Eidu at all. That Mohinder Pratap knew the man could only have come from first-hand memory.

We turned into Krishna Street and there, sitting on the threshold and preparing vegetables for the evening meal, was the virago.

'Bhaiji,' I complained, 'this woman does not let me look inside the house.'

'Oye, who do you think you are to not permit this man into his grandfather's home?' Mohinder Pratap, arms akimbo, asked the woman angrily. She looked up at him speechlessly, her knife hand frozen in mid-swipe across a wad of cilantro.

'Get out of the way,' he said, as he pushed her away with his foot almost in a manner of kicking. 'Go look. You have every right, more than this woman, to be in there,' he said to me.

For the first time I had free run of the home. I looked inside every room and even got to climb up to the roof without the woman screaming for me to get out. Mohinder Pratap joined me and we spent three quarters of an hour exploring the whole house. He said the small pediment-shaped device looking out to the street kept the Persian lettering for some years after Partition. It was then washed over and replaced with the Hindi, a faded impression of which still remains. That would have said 'Habib Manzil', I told him, named after Chan.

Mohinder Pratap did not remember either my father or Chan. He said both lived in Karachi. When he was growing up my father and uncle were studying one after the other at Government College, Lahore. They would have come home only in short snatches, not long enough for a pre-teen boy to register. One subsequently went to Roorkee and the other remained in Lahore at King Edward Medical College (now University).

But Mohinder Pratap did remember my aunts, especially that they went up on the roof at the end of each month of fasting to scan the western horizon for the new moon heralding Eid.

On the roof, I asked if this was from where the child was pitched to his death. He said it had all happened in the home of the Chopras. But that could not be, I argued.

'My grandfather and Lala Bheek Chand were friends. The family would either have been in their own home or in the protection of Lalaji.'

'Everyone knew of your grandfather's and Lala ji's friendship. Had the mob not found doctor sahib and his family in their own home, they would surely have proceeded then to Lala Bheek Chand's home and would have ordered him to stand aside,' said Mohinder Pratap.

Doctor sahib and his family were hidden in the Chopras' home where no one could suspect their presence, he said, as we went down the stairs and turned left along the wall of Habib Manzil.

'This was Eidu's room,' he pointed to a green door in the wall of Habib Manzil. The memory from countless times of seeing Eidu and his children emerge from that door had not dimmed in six decades.

The roaring, baying mob turned from Railway Road into Krishna Street. Among those in the lead was Mohinder Pratap's father. The roar grew and Eidu panicked. His wife and the four older children were already with my grandparents, and he knew they were in the Chopras' home. The man gathered up his two-year-old boy and bolted out of the room. As he turned into the street at the end of which Mohinder Pratap lived with his family, the senior Sehgal leading the mob made after him and saw him disappear into the Chopras' door. We turned right into the gated alley, the way Eidu sprinted that humid August long ago. The Chopra home was the fourth or fifth on the left. As we paused outside after knocking, I could almost hear the mob behind us.

Eidu may have tried the door of the room where my family cowered, and finding it bolted from inside, he ran up the stairs. Just then the senior Sehgal ducked into the courtyard and pursued him to the roof. There he knifed Eidu repeatedly and then pitched his infant son into the courtyard below. At that moment, the leaders of the mob gathered outside the room where my grandfather Dr Badaruddin, his wife Fatima, their daughters Jamila and Tahira, and my grandmother's father Qutubuddin awaited their final moments together with Eidu's wife Fateh and their four little children.

Since that March day in 2008, I have wondered many times how they would have behaved faced as they were with certain and violent death. Would they have tasted the metallic taste of fear in the back of their throats? Would my aunts have wept? Grandmother Fatima is said to have been a woman of exceptional grit. Family lore has it that woken by some knocking about in the middle of night, she found a burglar making off with a trunk. All alone, she pursued the man into the street, smacked him hard on his back and as he stumbled, snatched the trunk off his head. Another smack sent the man running and she returned home with her property. She would have kept her cool telling her daughters to rely on God who, obviously, was no longer mindful of them. As deeply religious as they were, they would surely have attempted to find solace by reciting prayers. But it would have helped very little that day.

Mohinder Pratap says through a hole in the door a rifle (or a shotgun) was fired into the room. The projectile caught my grandfather in the eye and he died instantaneously. That would have been when uncontrolled wailing might have broken out in the room. By my narrator's account, the door was not smashed. Very deliberately they undid a panel at the top to reach in and slide down the bolt. The door was thrown open, a few men entered and methodically slashed with daggers and swords the ten people who had at that moment lost all hope of humanity returning to the souls of the mob.

That day the lives of twelve—five of my direct family and seven of Eidu's—blameless people came to a violent end to become a part of the statistic of over a million dead in the Partition riots. My grandfather was then sixty years old; my grandmother five years younger. Mian Qutubuddin, my great-grandfather would have been ninety, give or take a couple of years, and my aunt Jamila in her late twenties. Tahira, the baby of the family, was twenty-two.

While Mohinder Pratap and Iqbal Singh with his two sons waited in the courtyard, I entered the room in the middle of which sat a large vat fitted with kneading arms and an electric motor. Around the green-washed walls, now badly in want of repainting, rested sacks of refined flour. In silence I gazed at the walls that were once spattered with the same blood as mine. Where would have they huddled hoping to dissolve into the brick and mortar behind them? Where my grandfather's body would have lain in its pool of blood? What were their final thoughts?

I felt nothing. If I had thought such a discovery would flood me with grief and I would weep uncontrollably, it did not happen. Not wanting my friend Ramneek to witness any emotional outburst, I had needlessly prevented his presence and had been glad when he returned to Rohtak after his short visit.

When I rejoined them in the courtyard, Mohinder Pratap was telling the others of the two-year-old child being pitched into the very courtyard where we stood. I asked the man of the house if he was a Chopra. He was not. He said the family sold this property decades ago and moved away from Jalandhar. We thanked the man and went out into the street.

I asked Mohinder Pratap to tell me truthfully what he knew of the fate of my aunts Jamila and Tahira.

'No living body left this room,' he said solemnly. 'After they were done with the dastardly deed, the rioters carted away the bodies on a barrow and cremated them at the firewood store in Railway Road very near where Kailash keeps business.'

Later Kailash Sehgal confirmed there was a taal—firewood store—owned by Pathans, adjacent to his family's property where many Muslim dead were unceremoniously burned. He spoke of having heard from his elders that the stench of burning and rotting flesh was so overpowering as to make life unbearable in Railway Road and other Muslim majority areas for many days and nights.

Chan had once told me that he remained at his intern's post with Irwin Hospital until October when he was finally airlifted to Lahore. Sometime in September the hospital learned that Punjab was facing a medical emergency with every danger of outbreak of pestilence because of the large number of decomposing corpses. As well as that, that part of the country was awash with refugees streaming in from the other side, many of them sick or wounded. Volunteers were asked for and my uncle opted to work in Jalandhar. Once there, he met with the settlement commissioner to ask about Muslim refugees still in camps in the city.

There were none, he was told. The Muslims had all either been expatriated to Pakistan or were dead. Chan did not have the courage to go check out the Railway Road home for himself. Nor too could he get himself to see Lala Bheek Chand and get the final word. Surely deep inside Chan would not have wanted to be confronted with the horrible truth. He never said anything of the sort to me, but I feel he would have harboured the hope that his parents and sisters having been expatriated would be safe somewhere in Pakistan. For a month he tended ailing refugees who had paid for his country with their properties and the blood of their families even as he worried over the fate of his own.

Unasked, Mohinder Pratap tendered a damning bit of information. With Tahira's wedding in the works, the family had prepared a suitable dowry. He said the gold and the cash at home was carried by my grandfather when the family went into hiding. That was the logical thing to do for the house would certainly have been ransacked. The Chopras, he said, had their eyes on the bags. Once the deed was done, they became masters of whatever my grandparents had brought with them. But that may not be entirely how it happened. We know that most rioters looted and it is right likely that if there were any valuables in the room of the killing, mob leaders would have appropriated them.

'Bhai ji, you were only thirteen at the time of Partition. How could you have been in the mob? How do you know this in such detail?' I who was uncomprehendingly watching the fast-forward movie asked.

'What? You've not been listening to me! I told you it was my father who led the mob.' Mohinder Pratap glared at me. Once again he used the words bevakoof and tung dil for the man. However, sanity returned within days, he said. Then the senior Sehgal began to rue his madness. His soul racked by guilt, the man would weep incessantly and say he committed a grave sin against very decent human beings. To emphasize, Mohinder Pratap repeated himself twice. He said his father remained repentant of his folly until his death in 1973.

Guilt riddles the soul. As it did in the case of Charan Singh of Buttar Kalan off the Grand Trunk Road between Amritsar and Jalandhar. There my friend, the late and much lamented Punjabi writer Talwinder Singh, drove me on a foggy morning in mid-January 2010 to meet the eighty-three-year-old man. Even before his grandson led him into the courtyard of the house where we waited, we heard the tap-tap-tap of Charan Singh's walking stick. Slightly built of medium height, old Charan Singh had milky white eyes that had not seen light for twenty years.

In 1947, as a twenty year-old sepoy in the district administration, he was assigned at Kasur as security guard to a Sikh revenue officer when Partition was announced. According to Charan Singh, this officer tried every which way for Kasur to be part of India, but what was a mere revenue officer when the powers that were wanted the city to go to Pakistan. And so, one day all Hindu and Sikh officers attended office for the last time and prepared to head east for Khem Karan, the nearest town of the new, divided India.

On the way, they crossed the BRB canal and Charan Singh recalls seeing it virtually clogged with dead bodies: men, women, and children alike. These were those luckless Hindus and Sikhs who had only a few days earlier lived peaceably with their Muslim neighbours in nearby villages.

'My mind was filled not with grief seeing the dead, but with rage and an overpowering desire for revenge,' he recalled.

Deserting his post, young Charan Singh reached home in Buttar and joined the mobs running amok across the country. They killed and looted, their hearts bursting with religious fervour and indignation at the needless and brutal deaths of their co-religionists in Pakistan. There was no remorse, no twinge of guilt upon doing in a fellow human being for no part in the grisly events occurring in the west. It was, he said, as if men had descended to a level below the lowliest beasts. As more and more trainloads of dead Sikhs and Hindus arrived, the call to exact greater vengeance charged up Charan Singh. To add to this were the tales told by those lucky to have lost only their worldly possessions and made it across the border with their lives.

Charan Singh said it was religious fervour that made him join the rampaging mob. It was passion whipped up by religious leaders in the name of God that made him kill the very same people who had amicably shared the village with him. He said his blood had turned white and he lost count of the number of people he killed. Many of these were neighbours to whom his family sent food on the Lohri festival and who in turn sent them vermicelli or meat depending on which Eid it was.

On one occasion the mob he was with filled up three bullock carts with the dead to dump in the Beas River that flows a few miles eastward of Buttar Kalan. This macabre convoy was followed by the women who had survived the killing of their men folk. Charan Singh did not mention how the women may have already suffered but he said he and the others offered them life and security if they would care to live with Sikh families.

'But those women were of a strange mettle. Not one of those more than one hundred agreed to convert.'

On the banks of the Beas, already swollen by Bhadon rains and dead bodies, the carts were tipped over one by one. As the bodies splashed into the brown eddies, the women jumped in after their dead kin.

'Not one of them lived,' said Charan Singh. 'They went into the water without a sound; without a cry or a curse hurled at us, we who had wronged them so terribly.'

Old Charan Singh took a deep sigh and fell silent, his head down, his eyes staring sightlessly at his hands in his lap. I do not know if he shed a tear or even if his dead eyes still possessed the capacity to weep, but a tortured gasp escaped his lips before he turned his sightless eyes up again.

'This great sin was wrought by our religious leaders. It was they who urged us to kill and avenge our brothers,' he said. 'Now I pay for my crime against humanity. My sight has gone because I sinned against my own brothers. I killed without remorse and now the Parmatma punishes me. What is life with sightless eyes? I have suffered this miserable life for twenty years and do not know how much longer I must live.' But in the heat of that madness, Charan Singh had felt no regret. Remorse only set in some time after.

Back home in Lahore, my friend Iqbal Qaiser, a Punjabi intellectual and expert on Pakistan's Sikh religious heritage, had a similar story to tell from the village of Laliani near Kasur. Some years earlier, he interviewed an elderly man in that village who told him of two men who shared the time of Partition. One Jalal or Jala, as he was known, of the caste Teli (Oil Presser) and the other Zaildar Sardar Anant Singh Bhullar. Jala Teli, a feared hoodlum, ran a gang of four whose depredations became more and more fearsome as the hour of the division of the land drew nigh. One of the members of this gang was the ruthless Karim Buksh also of the Teli caste from whose brother Iqbal heard the tale. Karim Buksh, it was said, had died a sorry, repentant man. Blind and crippled for many years before death finally overtook him, the man rued his part in the killings that oversaw Partition. His dying lament was that his end was miserable because of the sins he committed against humanity as a member of the Jala Teli gang.

Now, Laliani was a predominantly Sikh village. The only non-Sikhs were the Telis and Kumhars (potters)—both so-called 'low castes'—besides a number of Christian families. There were also some landed Muslim families of the Bhullar caste who had converted sometime in the seventeenth century. As the owner of, reportedly, some two thousand acres of agricultural land, Sardar Anant Singh was the big man in the village and among the richest persons in the district. More than that, he was a man who possessed a kindness and largesse of the spirit that knew no bounds and which transcended all considerations of caste and creed.

The story that Karim Buksh's brother narrated to Iqbal has it that one day this good man was out on his horse when he came upon a young and apparently newly-wedded couple. Who were they, he asked, and where were they headed? The man replied that he, a Christian of village Katloi, was a son-in-law of Laliani and was on his way to take his bride visiting her family. Sardar Anant Singh dismounted, helped the young woman onto his horse and taking the reins in his hands led the couple straight to his home.

There this man of God gifted the couple a mare, a buffalo, and new sets of clothing just as he would his own son-in-law on his first visit after the wedding. Having fed them, he then had them escorted to the bride's home. That was not all, said Iqbal Qaiser. The mosque known even today as Adday wali Maseet owes everything to the good Sardar. He got his kinsmen, the Muslim Bhullars, to donate the land for the mosque and paid for the building of the structure from his own wealth. It was also said that there was scarcely a family in Laliani that had not at some time or the other availed of the kindness of Sardar Anant Singh. Such was the goodness of that man.

When the riots began, the police post of Laliani was in the charge of a Muslim inspector. Greatly prejudiced against non-Muslims, this man instigated Jala Teli and his gang to have their way with the Sikhs, assuring them that he and his force would stand aside. When rioting started, the inspector invited Sardar Anant Singh to his police station to discuss expatriation procedures for Sikh families even as he treacherously informed the miscreants of the Sardar's possible movement. There, outside the police station, Jala and his cohorts awaited the arrival of the good man. And there, in full view of the police force as well as of so many others who had benefited from his munificence, Karim Buksh and Jala attacked and slew Sardar Anant Singh Bhullar.

With him gone, chaos descended upon the Sikh community. Leaderless and surrounded by mobs baying for blood, they sought refuge in the local gurudwara. Jala Teli and his three accomplices leading a large mob set the temple alight. All those who had taken refuge in the house of worship perished in the flames. I do not know if it was good fortune or the injustice of Providence that Anant Singh's family had already been expatriated to India, there to grieve the death of that humane and benevolent person.

Karim Buksh Teli passed away blind and crippled and it is entirely my loss that I missed him by many years. Iqbal Qaiser who interviewed his brother Meraj Din, who died in April 2008, said he was tormented by grief and shame for what he had done during the riots. Like Charan Singh in Buttar Kalan, Karim Buksh was convinced that his blindness and chronic caducity resulting in the inability to even attend to his various needs by himself was divine retribution.

On the authority of Meraj Din, Iqbal reported that Jala Teli and his three associates all died miserable, painful deaths, seeking forgiveness for the sins they had committed against their fellow citizens. Like Karim Buksh, Jala too was blinded and crippled in his last years. And when he would not die and his sons wearied of tending to the old man, they turned him out of the house. Jala Teli who may or may not have availed of the benevolence of Sardar Anant Singh, but who surely had denied others the chance to continue to benefit from this man's goodness, died on the streets of Laliani, unloved and untended, weeping in his final days over the sins he had committed during the riots of Partition.

To have slain a man of such kindness and generosity as Anant Singh must have taken callousness and barbarity of the meanest strain. I missed Karim Buksh and Jala Teli by some years and could not hear their stories in their own words. But I would dearly have liked to ask them if they, like Charan Singh, also held the political and religious leaders of their time responsible for fomenting this hatred.

SIX

Providence let off Mohinder Pratap's father lightly. I wonder if, like Charan Singh, he too was charged up because of the massacre in west Punjab. If not, it may be that he held some sort of rancour against my grandfather. Could it be that he had not been satisfied by the good doctor's ministrations? Or had he been slighted by Dr Badaruddin in some manner? If the teller of my tale knew anything of this sort, he did not pass it on.

He, Mohinder Pratap Sehgal, son of a man who died with the blood of my family on his hands and whose name I never asked, a Hindu, and I, born into a family of devout Muslims, stood there in the bright late afternoon sunshine looking at each other as we tried to come to grips with what had just been narrated. I felt no emotion; nothing against the teller of my family's story. If anything, I was overcome by Mohinder Pratap's use of the phrase 'our doctor sahib' for my grandfather. It bore a feeling of intimacy rooted in what he knew of the man even though, as he said, he had never been treated by him.

Even if this meeting had spooled at a fast-forward mode for me, my mind must have taken in his opening indictment of his father and apology on his behalf. Though I did not realize it then, I must have known that this good man endured in his heart the guilt of an error of judgement of his father's. If I had inherited grief from a family that never spoke explicitly of the loss suffered during Partition, Mohinder Pratap had a legacy of remorse from a father who rued his error to the end of his days. For a few moments neither of us spoke. I almost made to hug him, but something restrained me. I might have been afraid of his reaction though as I write now, eight years after that meeting, I know we both needed each other to heal our wounds of Partition. I had not let memory turn grief into hatred for them across the border. Instead, it taught me to forgive and move on. Mohinder Pratap had in the same way kept the guilt of his father, hoping perhaps to someday meet someone to apologize to. Our need for the other was mutual.

Almost two years after my first meeting with him, Shabnam and I were in Jalandhar together to see him on a cold December Sunday. We bore gifts for him: a Sindhi ajrak and cap. We did not want to take anything Punjabi, for we share the same things on either side of the border. Mohinder Pratap was delighted when we told him he did not have to use the ajrak himself and that a young girl in the family could have it stitched into a shirt.

Thereafter on three following visits to Jalandhar I made it a point to see him. We never spoke of Partition again for there were other things to talk of. We never asked each other how our exchange had helped the other. We did not need to ask if the balm of the meeting and our frank exchange had helped ease or even erase the pain and the guilt of that far-off event.

Mohinder Pratap did not live long after our last meeting in 2010. In July or August 2012, when I asked Iqbal Singh on the phone to convey my best wishes to him, I was told that the good man had shortly before passed away. Two years earlier, Pundit Fakir Chand Sangar had also died. My last remaining link with my grandfather was lost.

◆

Bal Krishna of Amritsar, the retired guard on the North Western Railway who chaperoned the last refugee train east from Ganda Singhwala railway station to Ferozepur, told me the story of what could have been a porous border—exactly as my grandfather had envisioned. Tragically it never came to pass. The pipe-fitters of Amritsar were all Muslims, he said. With their mass exodus to Lahore, the city of Harmandir Sahib was left without a man to tend to plumbing problems. By and by, a method was evolved: a cyclist would ride out the 50 kilometres from Amritsar to Lahore with a list of tasks needing attention and the following day a cavalcade of pedalling plumbers would head out for Amritsar with their tools to earn a day's honest wage. If I am to believe Bal Krishna, this state of affairs continued for about three years after Partition!

There are only two ways this could have happened. It is possible the migrating pipe-fitters left behind addresses where the Amritsari messenger could reach them. But more likely, knowing the difficulty his erstwhile clients would be facing, it is possible that after the madness died down, one stout fellow braved the journey back to the old hometown to see how they fared. He would have been deluged with demands for service and the method evolved. The three years that this cross-border service continued was enough to train talented men in Amritsar.

But the border remained largely porous until the 1965 war. Thereafter the security state that Pakistan quickly became clamped down hard and Punjab suffered. Indeed, it is only Punjab that suffered, first during Partition and then again with the Iron Curtain falling across the border.

Residents of districts of Balochistan bordering Iran can freely travel across the border by acquiring a rahdari—right of passage—from the office of the deputy commissioner or his assistant. The same is good for Iranians. Likewise the districts of Khyber-Pakhtunkhwa abutting Afghanistan. It is another thing, however, that Pathans on either side of the border care not a whit for the document and generally come and go as they please. Similarly, the people of Gilgit-Baltistan and Xinjiang province in China have a free run of the other country with a rahdari. In no case is a visa needed. The same facility was denied to Punjab on both sides of the border. If anything, this is injustice piled upon the injury of 1947. But this was something that had to be done: an open border and free bilateral travel would have given the lie to the Two Nation Theory. It would have negated the very creation of Pakistan.

◆

Thankfully for me the generation that harped on the 'immense sacrifices Muslims rendered for Pakistan' has passed. We no longer hear this slanted phrase. I could have told them that it was not Muslims alone who sacrificed for Pakistan. There were as many—if not more—Hindus, Jains and Sikhs who, being economically way better off in west Punjab than the Muslims of the east, forfeited much more for us to have Pakistan. But that is a loss we prefer to ignore.

If the Indian government quickly formulated procedures for claims of property from incoming refugees, Pakistan did nothing of the sort. A zamindar like Sardar Mangal Singh of Haveli Mehan Singh in Gujranwala gave up 600 acres of canal-irrigated prime farmland to recover but a fraction of his wealth in India.* Incoming refugees from Punjab and from even further east were quickly allocated assets commensurate with bogus claims of vast properties wherever they filed their papers. Unlike India where there was not much abandoned property to go by, Pakistan, had a surfeit of rich lands and huge mansions left by fleeing zamindars and businessmen. Pakistan swiftly became a free-for-all real estate Mecca.

Even as incoming refugees enriched themselves with abandoned assets, natives broke into evacuee properties to become their owners—some of these properties were the very ones they had volunteered to protect until the madness passed and the real owners could return to reclaim them. But within days of the great divide, everyone knew that those who had departed were never returning.

The Pakistani bureaucracy became part of this culture of plunder. Years ago, my friend Mazhar Zaidi, film-maker and writer, told me a very significant story that serves as a dishonorable epitome of what the country became so swiftly. He had heard from a retired bureaucrat who was either himself

---

*In March 2010, my friend Pargat Singh Grewal of Ludhiana took me to the home of a Bhinder Jat whose Muslim side of the family resides in Gujranwala. He put me in telephonic contact with Sardar Mangal Singh's octogenarian daughter. She corrected me: in Gujranwala I had been told that the Sardar owned 3,000 acres.

Salman Rashid

the settlement commissioner or had worked with that office in Lahore in 1947–1948. The man said, so Mazhar related, anyone with keys in their possession claiming those could open locked properties abandoned east of the new border were allotted as many havelis as they had keys. This meant, I remember remarking to Mazhar, that a bunch of keys dropped perhaps right outside the commissioner's office by a panic-stricken departing refugee and found by anyone was the finders' key to riches they had never known. That was true, Mazhar said. Only the commissioner's office wanted confirmation that the claimant had come from the other side. I laughingly called Pakistan chabi wala mulk— literally, a wind-up toy country.

I could laugh, for I was younger and I had not yet experienced the pain of men like Sardar Saudagar Singh in Ughi or Darshan Singh in Jalandhar. Nor too did I know of the loss of Sardar Mangal Singh and his children. And, because of their studied silence, I even knew little of the grief of my own family. Now I only feel a sense of shame for what we have become. The connotation of my phrase was, and still is, disparaging for it shows how easy enrichment had suddenly become for the poor and the venal. It was as if Pakistan was created as a short cut to wealth for not so rich Muslims. Affluence was not an outcome of years of hard toil; for refugees and natives alike in the new Pakistan, this sudden enrichment was windfall. We became a society in mutation, not evolution: it destroyed the people's psyche and shredded the social fabric of the new country. We quickly became a nation of upstart show-offs.

Evil is learned swiftly; goodness takes generations to become part of one's consciousness. Short cuts became our preferred way of life. Whether we walk or drive or seek wealth and fame, we devise short cuts. What was easily acquired during the unsettled years immediately after Partition, taught Pakistanis to live by flash. And this was not the affliction of common people alone. Successive governments did little better. A fine example of this is how the country has always squandered foreign loans on unnecessary luxuries worth millions of rupees.

If they are not frittering away loans on useless toys, our politicians, both civil and military, and the equally corrupt bureaucracy squirrel away vast sums in foreign bank accounts. When America's jihad against Soviet Russia in Afghanistan pumped in billions of US dollars into the country, much of it ended up in private bank accounts. We know of sons of military politicians of the 1980s (exterminated in an auspicious though much belated air crash) who now themselves dabble in politics and boast of vast business or agricultural empires. One of them is known to have privately ridiculed the other for fewer assets particularly since the latter's father was the senior and had greater access to funds to pilfer. Before they took to politics in uniform, their fathers—both refugees from Jalandhar—had the means of ordinary generals, which in those days were not much.

We learned all the wrong lessons from Partition. If we learned to be swayed so easily by the base lust for lucre, we also internalized the savagery and violence accompanying the creation of Pakistan. Within years we inflicted it upon compatriots who differed in their interpretation of our common religion. First our target was fellow Muslim Bengalis. Blameless women, men and children were under fire only because they were short of stature, dark and 'Hinduized' and therefore inferior to us. They were deemed unsuitable to rule over us even if principles of democracy gave them that right.

The same bias led us Punjabis to visit injustice upon Sindhis in the 1980s. In January 1988, working on a government of Sindh assignment, Shabnam and I travelled extensively in the outback of Dadu district among other areas of the province. Those were days when law and order had completely broken down and rural Sindh was in the grip of outlaws who kidnapped and plundered at will and the army was called in to fight them. In order to ensure our safety, the deputy commissioner organized an escort for us whenever we went into the interior.

One afternoon we were driving across an utterly unpopulated scrub desert looking for a seventeenth-century funerary monument and not finding it. At one point we came across a man on a bicycle. Even before I could roll down my window and hail him, the army subedar of our escort, a Punjabi from Chakwal, riding in the back seat had done it.

'Oye! Come here, you!' he barked and the poor cyclist almost froze with terror. He dismounted, let his bicycle fall to the ground, saluted and just stood there immobilized with fear.

When we were done with the poor man, I said to our subedar sahib his behaviour was exactly what had alienated the Bengalis. Now it was the turn of the Sindhis. The man shocked me when he said they deserved to be treated like this for they too were Hinduized. He was referring to the Sindhi custom of joining the hands in greeting.

At that same time we were finding newer and newer bugbears to feed our latent savagery. The military dictator bequeathed us laws and terrorist organizations to persecute religious minorities, even minorities within our common religion. Unheard of until the 1980s, slayings of Ahmedis and Shias became commonplace and continue to this day. There is no gainsaying that assassins are seldom caught and even more rarely prosecuted. And when they are, the trials are sham. For one, the police build a slipshod case so that the investigating officer is not later executed by the terrorist organization behind the religion-based murder. Secondly, witnesses fearing the same fate refuse to testify. To top it all, judges terrified for their lives let off terrorists. Nevertheless, we also know of police officers losing their lives for the work they did against terrorists. And we know of at least one judge, a man of courage and principle, who had to flee the country after sentencing the murderer of governor Salmaan Taseer. In October 2011, Judge Pervez Ali Shah fled to the Middle East upon receiving death threats and to this day reportedly lives in Saudi Arabia.

As if that violence was not sufficient to satisfy the blood lust we inherited at the time of Partition, we next took on the people of Balochistan. Once again those liberal and the only truly secular people among us were labelled lesser Muslims and even less Pakistanis. The kill-and-dump policy followed by army-led law enforcement agencies may have eliminated a few separatist rebels but in a larger measure it wholly targets blameless Baloch youth. In 2007, I knew things were out of control when a Baloch friend said it had 'become difficult to be a Baloch'.

In those days of Partition lawlessness we also learned that the state as represented by the white man no longer existed. If we feared its power in the 1950s, it was only a hangover of colonial times. By the 1960s, it had completely worn off. In 1968, phone boxes were installed on The Mall and in Gulberg in Lahore. As in the West, each was equipped with a telephone directory besides the pay phone. Within twenty-four hours of installation, the phone books were stolen. Next the microphones and speakers in the handsets went. In less than a week, only the empty phone boxes, stripped of all fittings, remained. After the plunder of 1947, we got the second taste of how exciting life could be when the state abdicated all responsibility. Hence onward, there was no stopping.

In 1974, on leave from the army, I one night accosted three men removing newly installed cats' eyes from a road in Gulberg. When I asked them why, they laughingly said the lights would look pretty in their home. Little did they know that the eyes only shone on reflected light. Things got ugly when I told them to desist and I had to beat a hasty retreat when they menacingly brandished their screw drivers, pliers and a couple of hammers.

Plastic or wooden seats installed in bus stops are routinely vandalized. Iron railing on road dividers to prevent jaywalking under an overhead pedestrian bridge is always cut and removed to make way so that climbing the bridge can be avoided. Concrete blocks of road dividers are routinely smashed to create a gap and permit shortcuts for motorcyclists regardless that they cut dangerously across speeding traffic. All these things of course cannot be done in a few minutes. They require hours of manual labour by not a single individual but quite a number of persons. Yet these projects of rampant vandalization are executed on the busiest streets of Lahore, in many cases right outside police stations.

It is as if Pakistan is under enemy occupation and its people bent upon causing as much damage to the occupiers as is within their power. When they are at their patriotic undertaking, no civic-minded person dare stop the vandalism. And officialdom simply could not care any less.

We learned in the Partition riots that the law meant nothing when we killed, raped and looted mindlessly. Today the children of those same plunderers and rapists re-enact the black deeds of that turbulent time with impunity. In years I have never heard anyone expressing fear of the police when they, say, jump a red light. Everyone openly and without fear of penalty does everything that is against the law, for they know in Pakistan the state does not exist.

In March 2010, as my friend Pargat Singh Grewal drove me around Ludhiana he pointed out across the concrete divider to the far side of the road the side lane we needed to take. The U-turn was about fifty metres away and just to test him, I told him to get on the wrong side of the road through the cut in the divider—something that is the norm in Pakistan. He was aghast. Why, the police would fine him for the misdemeanour. Pargat, a man of my age, who had retired shortly before from a government assignment, was afraid of the law. Surely something was being done right in India. Something that we should have emulated if we had any sense at all. But we do not follow an 'enemy country'.

We did however learn one lesson right. Jinnah said, 'Every successive government [in Pakistan] will be worse than its predecessor'. Leaders and commoners of the Quaid-e-Azam's Pakistan made this utterance of his their guiding principle and we have seen a steady and unstoppable decline in governance, bureaucracy and military leadership. The intellectual decay is widespread, for we find progressively feeble-minded and immature persons rising to the top. They say we are ruled by the cream of the nation. To me it seems more like scum riding the flow of a sewer.

SEVEN

'Why did this have to happen?' I asked on that March afternoon as we stood sheltering from the sun in the gated corner of Krishna Street. Mohinder Pratap looked me squarely in the eye for a moment.

'It was a time of great madness,' he said simply.

It was madness unleashed by politicians who had no clue as to what they were doing. I am no historian, I understand neither politics nor modern political history. I am therefore quite unlettered in the details of the Pakistan Movement. In Ughi, Pundit Fakir Chand had said 'something' had occurred in the early 1940s that transformed my grandfather. Other than my grandfather joining the Muslim League, he was unable to tell me anything more. Dr Badaruddin could not have been a fist-waving, slogan-chanting activist, for that was simply not part of our family as I can tell from what I know of my father and Chan. All he would have done was to have aligned himself with the party and the demand for a separate country for the Muslims of India—even though he had every intention of continuing to live in his native Jalandhar.

In early 2016, talking to I. A. Rehman I received information hitherto unknown to me. It gave me an understanding of my grandfather's transformation as well as the nature of the animosity in the years leading up to Partition. A renowned human rights and peace activist for which he won the 2004 Magsaysay Award for Peace and International Understanding, Rehman is a brilliant public speaker, a great storyteller and a man possessed of a scintillating sense of humour. He is one of the most admirable characters I have known in my life.

He said the politics of the twentieth century had, by the late 1920s, deeply communalized Indian society.* Earlier, professional people, with the exception of Sikhs, generally dressed and conducted themselves in a way to *not* give away their religious identity. But after the rift was created, it became essential to proclaim one's creed openly. If earlier nepotism for a job opening began and ended with someone being from one's village, it now went one step further to consider religion foremost.

Pundit Fakir Chand had remembered my grandfather as a man who entertained visitors on equal terms regardless of religion and domicile. That meant that he had somehow kept himself from the communalism for some considerable time. But by the early 1940s he too had succumbed to it as we know from the case of the Sikh with the bee stuck in his ear. Likewise, the attempt to slaughter a cow in Ughi was manifest mischief to perhaps verify his power in the last year of his government service. As a native of a Muslim majority district his confidence

---

*This is also confirmed by Rajmohan Gandhi's *Punjab: A History from Aurangzeb to Mountbatten*. This book is essential reading for the student of modern history focusing on Punjab and Partition.

may also have rested upon the notion that Jalandhar would perhaps be part of Pakistan.

By religious law, while much of it is distributed among family, friends and the poor, a portion of the flesh *has* to be consumed by the maker of the offering. No one in our family was going to overcome their abhorrence of beef in order to keep the Islamic injunction. This much my grandfather would also have known. But the cow had to be killed even if only to rile up the side that was now enemy. Though at this stage no one can either confirm or deny it, I am certain that for the family's consumption a goat would also have been killed in the privacy of the home.

The early 1940s was a time when Congress leaders had embarked on their 'fill the jails' campaign and were all, including the working committee, behind bars. On the other hand, Muslim League leaders were free to play footsie with the Raj. They were free to indulge in their politics and 'educate' their followers as they saw fit. So far as I know there are no documentary details of what lower echelon leaders were doing to followers like my grandfather, but from his altered behaviour I get a fair idea: Muslim League leaders were busy fanning communalism to bolster their Two Nation Theory. It seems these leaders either did not comprehend or simply did not care where such a philosophy would eventually lead. In the first case, they were incompetent; utterly out of their depth. In the second, they can only be accused of criminality.

These district level leaders were taking their cue from the proclamation of Mohammad Ali Jinnah in his presidential address during the Lahore Resolution of 24 March 1940:*

> Hindus and Muslims belong to two different religious philosophies, social customs and literature. They neither inter-marry nor inter-dine together, and, indeed, they belong to two different civilisations that are based mainly on conflicting ideas and conceptions. Their concepts on life and of life are different. It is quite clear that Hindus and Muslims derive their inspiration from different sources of history. They have different epics, different heroes and different episodes. Very often the hero of one is a foe of the other, and likewise, their victories and defeats overlap. To yoke together two such nations under a single state, one as a numerical minority and the other as a majority, must lead to growing discontent and final destruction of any fabric that may be so built up for the government of such a state.

Just seven years later, Jinnah's address to the Constituent Assembly of Pakistan blatantly contravened the last part of the above statement. On 11 August 1947, the Governor General famously, in a now oft-quoted speech, told the people of the new country that they were free to go to their temples, mosques or any other places of worship for one's religion, caste or creed had nothing to do with the business of the state. He went on to assert that following these principles in Pakistan, 'Hindus would cease to be Hindus and Muslims would cease to be Muslims, not in the religious sense, because that is the personal faith of

*For some reason, 'Pakistan Day' is celebrated on 23 March and not the following day when the resolution was passed.

Salman Rashid

each individual, but in the political sense as citizens of the state.'

One does wonder what became of the 'destruction of the fabric' of the state under these circumstances that had so concerned Jinnah only seven years earlier. (My copy of *Speeches*, an undated government publication from the 1950s, contains the 11 August address in full. However, the military dictator [1977–88] expunged this speech from reprints during his misrule.)

Had he so wished, a leader as charismatic as Jinnah could have taken an opposing view to steer his flock away from such divisiveness. Instead, resting upon communalism, the Two Nation Theory was nurtured by Jinnah only after he was politically sidelined by Mahatma Gandhi and rebuffed by Muslim religious leaders in the 1920s. After years in the wilderness, he changed tack and abandoned his championship of Hindu-Muslim unity. The theory was created two hundred years after a thousand year-long Muslim domination of India had ended. One wonders why such a notion did not exist in, say, the seventeenth century or before when Islam was the religion of the ruling class. However, to be fair to Jinnah, in his speech, part of which is quoted above, he referred to a purported letter by Lala Lajpat Rai to Chittaranjan Das, the Bengali nationalist leader. In this letter written in 1924, we are told, Rai was explicit that as two distinct nations, Hindus and Muslims could never be reconciled.

History tells us that communal relationships were not as bleak, however. Only four years before the writing of that letter, following the vile massacre of 379 unarmed non-violent protestors and Baisakhi revellers (some 1100 wounded) in Amritsar's Jallianwala Bagh, India had witnessed a remarkable Hindu-Muslim-Sikh unity after Gandhi called for non-cooperation with the Raj. This concord lasted until the end of 1921 when Lala Lajpat Rai in a letter on record wrote: 'It is a fact that from 1919 to the end of 1921 Hindus and Muslims of India were fairly united... For the first time in the history of India, a Kafir preached from the pulpit of the biggest and historically... the most magnificent mosque of Northern India.'*

Lajpat Rai was referring to the April 1919 rallies in Punjab when the businessman and newspaper publisher Lala Harkishen Lal and Arya Samaj leader Rambhuj Dutt Chaudhuri addressed a congregation from the pulpit of Lahore's Badshahi Mosque. This was also a time when Hindu and Muslim leaders drank from the same cup, not just figuratively but in actual fact, and exchanged headgear.

This could have been a rerun of earlier unity as recorded in the Punjabi ballad of Shah Mohammad. The *Jangnama*, written shortly after the fall of the Sikh Empire, lamented the evil wrought by the white man. Admittedly, a close relative of the poet's, one Sultan Mahmud, was an artillery officer in the army of Maharaja Ranjit Singh and the family would have gained significantly from this position causing Shah Mohammad's vision to be somewhat bitter. The poetry nevertheless sings of trust between Sikhs and Muslims and it seems that during Sikh rule, the religious divide may not have been as strong as one might be led to believe.

According to Rajmohan Gandhi, the emergence in the 1880s of a number of Punjabi, Urdu and English language

---

*Rajmohan Gandhi's *Punjab: A History from Aurangzeb to Mountbatten*, p. 297.

journals representing the Singh Sabha, Arya Samaj and Muslim viewpoints, led to an expansion of the religious debate. Rather than mitigating the divide, political leaders on both side were bent on deepening it. It seems this was not without a nod from wily Raj officers: 'While Muslim, Arya Samajist, Sikh or Christian debaters strove to establish that theirs was the soundest faith on offer, the Raj took comfort from the fact that Muslims, Hindus and Sikhs were not thinking of a common platform.'*

Clearly the Raj had very obvious and even comprehensive plans for what it wanted and it was working to that end. Consider: Mohammad Iqbal, now Pakistan's national poet, was, at the turn of his century, writing nationalistic poetry declaring Hindustan as the finest place in the entire world. As well as that, as a proponent of unity across religions, his poetry accused both the mullah and the pundit of spreading ignorance and discord—a 'crime' for which he was roundly censured by the mullahs. But the years from 1905 to 1908 when he was in Britain changed everything for him. Iqbal returned home to become a champion of reclaiming Muslim glory. Unity was no longer his byword. One cannot but wonder what lessons his tutors in Britain taught him in those three years. But if the politics and philosophy of Mahatma Gandhi could bring about religious cohesion between the years 1919 to 1921, why could other political leaders not build upon it?

Muslim League leaders believed that the departure of the Raj and governance of India under a democratic system, as envisaged by the Congress, would disadvantage Muslims, they being a one-fourth minority. In order to win at politics, Muslim

---

*Ibid. p. 250.

League leaders drove the wedge of communalism ever deeper into the soul of Punjab. And not that Congress leaders did not match folly with folly. If Gandhi stood for non-violence, the others seemed to care little that their crowns of glory were to be paid for by the blood of millions of their compatriots.

I asked I. A. Rehman a question that has long rankled with me: why, in the seven years and five months between the passing of the Lahore Resolution and the creation of Pakistan, could Muslim League leaders not draft a constitution for the country whose creation they had embarked upon?

This question had been asked before, however. Rehman said that sometime after Partition, in a Muslim League convention which he attended, Ashiq Hussain Batalvi, general secretary Punjab Muslim League, faced a similar query. Batalvi said when the country's founding fathers led the struggle, they were looking out for independence. It was like building a house. At that time, they were not concerned with how the interior of the house was to be decorated. That design would come later after reflection and consideration.

To my mind this was as inane and shallow an analogy as could ever be made. These were supposedly great political leaders set upon a course to carve a separate country from within India and they had no programme for it. Seven years was time long enough for all the reflection and consideration that was needed to set the proposed country on its course. Aside: I had long laboured under the misguided illusion that a constitution bearing Jinnah's endorsement would have been sacrosanct. I thought no dictator could have mustered the nerve to scorn it as the 1973 constitution was scorned. I. A. Rehman assured me military usurpers would have given as much thought to Jinnah's constitution as they habitually did to the later ones.

On the same question, Jinnah maintained another view, however: that framing of the constitution was the right and privilege of an elected body. With hindsight this seems more than anything else a statement for the gallery. In reality, had the leaders drafted a constitution, differences would have arisen over the question of boundaries of the new country. And neither Jinnah nor the British or anyone else knew where the border was going to be drawn. Not even until Partition was just four weeks away. A major upheaval and a great geographical change was in the works and strangely the Punjab Boundary Commission with Cyril Radcliffe as its chairman was constituted on the last day of June 1947. It did not complete its work until the end of July.

I. A. Rehman thinks that the Muslim League leadership was afraid that with the coming into the open of the question of boundaries of Pakistan, their following would be adversely affected. If the Muslim population of a staunchly Muslim League district like Jalandhar was to learn that they were not going to be a part of Pakistan, it was more likely than not that they would shift loyalty. And so neither the question of the constitution nor that of the new country's boundaries was ever raised. There was just one unholy, bloody-minded haste to divide the country and be done with it. And damn those hapless, helpless people caught in the vortex of the violence that promised to accompany this upheaval.

It seems vision was universally blighted and everyone was in a hurry to get what should have logically waited a few more years. Mountbatten, who to my mind appears to be incredibly immature and even foolish—a moron who should have been tried for crimes against humanity and hanged—wanted to do the job and get out as quickly as possible. Jinnah wanted it done the soonest in view of his tuberculosis of the lungs that he knew was killing him, a fact which he skilfully kept from public knowledge. Nehru, grieving over the cutting up of Mother India, had come to a stage where he seemed to have stopped caring about the bloodshed that seemed certain to take place. The tragedy that was sure to oversee Partition seemed to be a concern only for Mahatma Gandhi. One man against millions was bound to lose.

The haste to divide India precipitated population transfer. Saner, steadier minds at work would have rendered this needless and sanguinary exodus unnecessary. If the one raison d'être for Pakistan was to be a Muslim majority country, it would have been just that even without expelling its Hindus and Sikhs. But if at all it had to be this way, it could have been properly supervised and conducted under protective military columns. Instead of abdicating their responsibility as they did, district officers and police should have been in place to see that no violence took place. Had that been, this Mother of all Holocausts would not have occurred.

Instead, Partition was midwifed in an exactly opposite manner. It was as if someone wished to teach the people of India a lesson for their impudence in demanding freedom from the Raj. I suspect that someone was Mountbatten who in the words of the contemporary historian Andrew Roberts was 'a mendacious, intellectually limited hustler, whose negligence and incompetence resulted in many unnecessary deaths'. Roberts goes on to state: 'Mountbatten deserved to be court-martialled on his return to London'.

Salman Rashid

The ambiguity concerning actual geographical limits of the new country cost my grandfather everything he had. My sister Rauha once told me on the authority of our Sakina khala that until a stage very near the final day, he believed that even after Partition there would be no problem travelling this way or that across the land as one had done for centuries before. He is reported to have said that if my father wished to live in Pakistan that was all right. He simply did not believe that an Iron Curtain would descend upon the land cutting off families on either side. Even less did he know that before that would come to pass, there would be dreadful slaughter and that he and his dearest would go into their long night so that a 'moth-eaten Pakistan'—as Jinnah once famously referred to it in frustration—could be created.

Even that would have been fine had our vision been right. With hard work and commitment we could have made something out of a country worse than moth-eaten and made the great sacrifice of 1947 worthwhile. But our vision was blighted. Beginning with the Objectives Resolution of Liaquat Ali Khan and down through the years, Pakistani leadership did everything wrong. One cursory look at the decline of every single state institution bears out this truth. The few giants of the early years after Partition all stand replaced by pygmies everywhere one looks.

At an indeterminate time very early in the history of Pakistan, those who did not believe in what Jinnah claimed to hold close to his heart, altered the motto spelled out by the founder of the country: 'Unity, Discipline and Faith'.*

Growing up as a child as the state became progressively more hypocritical, I was told our motto was Unity, Faith and Discipline. But for the millitary-mullah cabal entrenched into the body politic of the country immediately after Partition and progressively made stronger over the early decades of its existence, even that was not sufficiently adhering to the identity it wished for the country. The blighted dictatorship of the 1980s reversed the order of the motto laid down by Jinnah and it became Faith, Unity and Discipline. Even today, three decades after the dictator evaporated in a fireball above Bahawalpur skies, the corrupted motto tarnishes a hillside along Islamabad Highway between Rewat town and the capital. It is entirely another thing that these three words are no better than tripe so far as the multitude comprising the country is concerned.

The vision, if Muslim leaders had any, was afflicted by the very name they chose for the country. Pakistanis are led to believe that a certain Choudhry Rahmat Ali, a Muslim nationalist yearning for a separate country, had coined the word Pakistan while in London in the 1930s. We are told that it was an acronym for Punjab, Afghania (what is now Khyber-Pakhtunkhwa), Sindh and the 'stan' taken from Balochistan. What we are never told is why the first letter of Bengal was missing from this new title, particularly when Muslim majority East Bengal was envisaged as part of this dream country. The Bengalis were smart. They took the hint that they were never meant to be part of this new country and went their separate way.

Pakistan was never taken seriously by its leaders and the

---

*My copy of *Speeches*, p. 34.

eventual independence of Bangladesh seems to have been part of the works from the very beginning. By the mid-1960s Pakistan's captains knew the time of the split was close. Kamal Azfar, barrister, politician and governor of Sindh in the 1990s, reveals an item in *The Waters of Lahore*. It is a story of the leadership's detachment from the fate of Pakistan; it chills because it concerns a military dictator who one would believe to be the most patriotic among patriots.

Dictator Ayub Khan had then been in the driving seat for seven years when his ambassador-designate to Thailand, Hayat Junejo, called upon him before leaving for accreditation. In the course of the interview, the dictator asked him how long he thought East Pakistan was going to remain with the rest of the country. It is not known if Junejo had a clear notion regarding the future, but he hedged. He may have feared his president's ire should he speak a truth inimical to the country. Ayub cut short his discomfiture: 'Let me tell you. At the most ten years, maybe five. We have given East Pakistan a civil service and an army so that they do not need to be hand-in-glove with India when they are independent.' With that the interview was concluded.

Five years was all it took for Ayub Khan's prediction to come true.

A supposed patriot was at the helm of the country to foretell the shattering of his Quaid-e-Azam's dream and he predicted it with unsettling detachment. As the master of all he surveyed from Peshawar to Cox's Bazar—less the intervening Indian territory— he was not willing to so much as move a finger to right matters that had been permitted to go wrong since August 1947. He was only happy that an independent East Pakistan would not fall into India's lap. For the leader of a country begotten with untold 'sacrifices' this was a most remarkable attitude.

The highly respected journalist Khaled Ahmed tells a very curious tale regarding the name Pakistan, however. He writes that it was no stroke of original brilliance on Rahmat Ali's part. Rather, he amputated the name from Karakalpakstan, a region straddling Uzbekistan and Turkmenistan. But when Jinnah heard of it—even though until that point in time he had never proposed a name for the country he wished to establish—he dismissed it as a 'students' dream'.* But when it came time to appropriate a name for the country, Pakistan sounded nice enough since its connotation in Urdu and Persian is Land of the [Spiritually] Pure. This is ironical as ironical can ever be.

In the latter years of the third century BCE, the descendants of Alexander's general Seleucus Nikator, having taken over Afghanistan, expanded their influence eastward to annex what is today exactly Pakistan. 'High-born' Indians of the east considered the foreigners unclean and disparagingly referred to their area of influence as Mlechha Desa—Land of the Unclean. Even after the end of the Indo-Greek empire, as it is known to historians, through the long pageant of Parthian, Scythian and Kushan rule (again restricted to present-day Pakistan), the appellation continued in use. Today when I look around, I find that I still live in a Land of the Unclean.

According to a 2015 survey 67 per cent of Pakistanis yearn for public life to be guided by the principles of Islam and wish the infliction of Sharia upon the population—though it defies imagination what keeps those who pine for Sharia from practising it themselves without enforcement. Yet unrestrained these deeply

---

*Khaled Ahmed, 'A tale from Karakalpakstan', *Indian Express*, 21 March 2015.

religious people fib, filch, cheat, rape, murder, obscenely exhibit ill-acquired wealth, and are possessed of insatiable lust for worldly possessions—qualities which any half decent human would eschew and condemn and which, as Muslims love to proclaim loudly, Islam frowns upon. What can a people as venal, hypocritical and two-faced as a majority of my compatriots be but unclean. The Mlechha Desa of ancient times lives under the green and white flag adorned with the crescent and star.

This historical fact dovetails with the issue of the complete lack of a Pakistani identity—something we have never pondered upon. Had the founding fathers of Pakistan read classical geography they would not have had to invent a name for as ancient a land as we live upon. Little did they know that the word 'India' derives from Sindhu, the name the early Sanskrit speakers gave to the greatest river they had ever seen. Imagine a Central Asiatic horde accustomed only to piddling streams like the Syr Darya or the Oxus coming down the Suleman Mountains to the banks of a river swollen by spring thaws, its flow spreading to a distant unseen shore. For them it was the Sindhu—Great River or even the Sea.

In an ecstasy the Rig Veda celebrates this first meeting of man and river even as the poet remains undecided if this flowing 'seven and seven Sindhu...in [which] might surpasses all the streams that flow' is a man or a woman thing. In verse so spectacularly moving that it raises goose bumps and mists the eye, that ancient master sings the roar of the river likening it to the 'bellowing of a bull' that is lifted to the heaven above and how like calves running to their milk-laden mothers 'roaring rivers run' to the great Maha Sapta Sindhu. Oh, this, in its full splendour untamed by today's dams, was the '[m]ost active of the active, Sindhu unrestrained, like to a dappled mare, beautiful, fair to see'.*

Who would, having once read these celestial lines, not have fallen in love with the land of the Sindhu. And who would not have known that the ancient Persians interpolating the initial *s* with *h* changed the name of the river to Hindu. For the speakers of Avestan, the land of the Hindu became Hindustan more than two-and-a-half millenniums ago. In all this time, Hindu was a geographical entity. Never, until the latter Middle Ages, did it take on a religious connotation.

Late in the sixth century BCE, the Greek sea captain Skylax under orders of Darius the Great sailed down the river from the vicinity of Peshawar to the sea to map it. By Greek usage dropping the initial *h* and appending a terminal *s*, he called it Indus. On his tongue, the name of the land where the river flowed was India. If there was an India in the subcontinent, it was exactly where Pakistan now sits. If I am anything, I, a child of the Maha Sapta Sindhu, am the truest Hindu. Only the ignorant would have wished for a new name for the Land of the Sindhu. By this one unthinking act, the founders of the new country cut the umbilical tethering us to an ancient past. Adrift without that mooring, it was only a matter of time before we lost all sense of identity. One act of foolishness deprived a mass of people of a past and a name.

With the invention of a new name, the imperative was to plaster a palimpsest over ancient history in order to suitably alter it. This was done in the years following Partition: the country of Pakistan, history textbooks began to proclaim, was created in

---

Rig Veda, Book X, Hymn LXXV.

the year 711 CE when Mohammad bin Qasim invaded Sindh. If he was celebrated so too could the other robber barons of Turkish origin who plundered this rich country from the tenth century onward.

Confusion has many facets. Official historians write of the natives fighting against Alexander the Macedonian as being 'Pakistan Army'. However, when Muslim Arabs arrive, this 'Pakistan Army' magically disappears to be replaced by natives. It is only natural that a schoolchild reading such tripe should grow up utterly confounded.

These myopic policies left little room for the immature collective mind of Pakistani people to fathom the reality of their nationhood and nationality. To add to the confusion were those who went abroad to study in the 1950s and returned to narrate that so many in the West, particularly in America, did not know where Pakistan was located. Upon elaboration the usual response, as reported, was, 'Oh, so you are a part of India.' A whole nation was growing up baffled about its identity.

I have shown above how common Pakistanis destroy government installations of public utility and how everyone who gets a chance plunders this country. Consider this against the background of the Ghazva-e-Hind—Holy War against India— that fraudster mullahs tell us has to be waged sooner than later to convert the people of the entire subcontinent to the 'one and only true faith'. The Ghazva has begun. It began with the founding of Pakistan. Only, Pakistani Muslims, somehow convinced that they in reality live in India, are concerned less with converting the heathen of the land. This modern day Ghazva concentrates on plunder. And that which cannot be taken has to be destroyed. The worst distortion of our identity was yet to come, however.

With the opening up of the Middle East petro-dollar reservoir, untold multitudes of mostly illiterate labourers streamed from Pakistan to the Persian Gulf and Saudi Arabia. They returned home with their impressionable minds overwhelmed with a vague, unformed love of the Arabic language and everything Arabian as representing Islam. This synchronized perfectly with the already rampant desire to have been illegitimately sired by an imaginary being of Arab origin. The effort to turn Pakistan into Arabia began and was brought to fruition in the early 1990s. That year a mindless bureaucrat, also a claimant of Arab origin, supplanted dozens of mango trees, hundreds of years old, in a part of Lahore with useless date palms.

The stampede to destroy local flora and replace it with the date palm began for a herd of confused, ignorant people with an imported narrative that deprived them of a philosophical-historical connection with the land they lived upon. Every new government building erected since the early 1990s is adorned only with shade-less date palms. Across the country tens of thousands, perhaps more, of leafy shade trees have been destroyed and replaced by trees to make us look more and more like the Arabian desert. Ordinary people taking their cue from a government of fools are reinforcing the palm tree invasion, mindless of our need for shade trees in this hot country.

Meanwhile, the hordes of illiterate labourers whose toil transformed the Middle East returned home to become the middle class with a new and slanted awareness: in the holy language, their country was Al-Bakistan. The coup de grâce to the tattered sense of being Pakistani was delivered after the Pakistan Muslim League government took over in Punjab in 2008. Car registration plates reading Al-Bakistan were shamelessly encouraged in the province, allegedly with a nod from the provincial government and funding from a Persian Gulf state. A confounded mob, deprived of any sense of self or pride in nationhood, quickly took to this vulgar practice as exemplifying their 'Islamic' character.

Inexplicably, Punjabis who suffered the most in Partition and who should have inculcated the greatest national pride have actively embraced this trend and even started adding the crossed swords topped by a date palm as seen on the Saudi flag to their registration plates. However, the other three provinces have still to catch on to the sickness. Nevertheless, the doing in of Jinnah's and Iqbal's Pakistan, whose name we like to believe was devised by Choudhry Rahmat Ali, has begun.

It seems it now only remains for our regional languages as well as Urdu to be overhauled. I suppose it is only a matter of time that all sounds unpronounceable in Arabic will be expunged from our lexicons so that the Arab colonization of Pakistan is complete. So much for our independence and a Pakistani identity.

In the decades of writing, my reference to August 1947 as Partition with the upper case has been criticized. I say we never really became independent. From British control we speedily slid under American influence and within years became slaves to international monetary agencies that pumped in loans so that even as her leaders misappropriated the funds to enrich themselves beyond measure, Pakistan hurtled down the dark tube of debt-ridden perdition. Other than being powered by external loans, we have today virtually no working economy. Indeed, of this moment, as every single Pakistani is under a debt of close to Rs 100,000, we cannot be accused of doubting if our country will ever become a financial powerhouse.

Since the 1990s my country hurts under Saudi influence. Never lagging in monetary largesse to prop up the venal Sharif dynasty controlling the misfortunes of Pakistan, the Arabs are endeavouring to alter the very culture of the country. Right from the dictatorship of the 1980s, the ancient Persian linguistic influence on Urdu has been craftily arabized. The most noticeable change is the death of the Persian Khuda and the emergence of the Arabic Allah in the everyday idiom of the country. As well as that, Arab influence, the most pernicious external control in seven decades, threatens not only to alter the name of the country to Al-Bakistan, but also to turn its landscape into a desert where date palms are replacing indigenous flora. With the crop of spineless filchers masquerading as leaders, there is little hope of the Pakistani nation becoming independent to develop an identity and a sense of self to counter this trend.

The greatest tragedy of Pakistan is that this country, achieved after such immense sacrifices—sacrifices rendered not just by Muslims, but more by Sikhs, Hindus and Jains—could have been a model in seven decades. Instead, the civil-military establishment teaming with the clergy turned it into a basket case. In the second decade of the twenty-first century, Pakistan is the Sick Man of the World, ravaged by leaders whose abject mental vacuity and spinelessness is matched only by insatiable rapacity; leaders who covet public office not to serve but to plunder. With an exceptional and huge human resource, we have yet failed to make anything meaningful of the country that my family paid for so dearly.

As the generation that suffered directly during the Partition riots fades away from this life, the memory of that great loss ebbs from the collective Pakistani consciousness. Even when the memory was fresh, it inexplicably inspired so few to strive to steer this new country onto a very difficult path: the right path. Those who held power, whether they were directly affected by Pakistan's creation or had lived securely in areas that fell within its borders, were sleazy mercenaries whose only ambition was self-aggrandisement and enrichment. To serve themselves, the captains of Pakistan's destiny squandered every single chance the country had. Turning it into a security state low on the scale of social and human development, they made a holy mess of a good thing. Consequently, when the memory of Partition is forever expunged with the passing of my generation we will be left with no hope. The great tragedy will not be the loss of life and property in the upheaval of 1947. It will be that those sacrifices, never having inspired us, will all have been in vain.

◆

Mohinder Pratap Sehgal and Pundit Fakir Chand Sangar, my only two links with a part of my family I never got to know, have gone into the great beyond. My real link with that past is severed. Sardar Saudagar Singh Josan lives as my last connection with Ughi and Lamyaan di Patti where we once had a home. I am grateful to him for his affection and in equal measure to his sons, Bakhshish in particular, that this association will remain as long as I live.

I am grateful too to Mohinder Pratap for his heartfelt apology when we first met. We need more men like him on both sides of the border, men who have the moral courage to admit the wrong they or the generation before them perpetrated. We need also men, particularly in Pakistan, who can admit the errors of the past seven decades and begin to make amends. Only then will the border between two peoples dissolve. Only then will there be peace. Only then will we know that we are, after all, brothers.

ACKNOWLEDGEMENTS

This book would not have been possible without the encouragement and even coaxing of Usha and Rajmohan Gandhi. Having read my newspaper version of 2008 on the internet, these wonderful people met me in Lahore in March 2010 to say that my story was too powerful to be lost in some newspaper archives. I dallied and they kept at it. In January 2014, in Panchgani, Rajmohan extracted a promise from me that I will write the book that year. It took two years for the promise to come to fruition.

I am grateful to all the people who made my first ever journey in India meaningful. Most of them are mentioned in my story.

To my publisher David Davidar a special thanks for waiving the condition of the first two chapters and synopsis for approval—or rejection! To my editor Simar Puneet I am deeply indebted for looking at this work from the depth of her Punjabi heart.